THE CHAEBOL

THE CHAEBOL
(JAÉ BOL)
Korea's New Industrial Might

RICHARD M. STEERS
YOO KEUN SHIN
GERARDO R. UNGSON

1817

Harper & Row, Publishers, New York
BALLINGER DIVISION

*Grand Rapids, Philadelphia, St. Louis, San Francisco
London, Singapore, Sydney, Tokyo, Toronto*

International Standard Book Number: 0-88730-372-2

Library of Congress Catalog Card Number: 89-45774

Printed in the United States of America

Library of Congress Cataloging-in-Publication Data

Steers, Richard M.
   The chaebol : Korea's new industrial might / Richard M. Steers,
Yoo Keun Shin, Gerardo R. Ungson.
   Includes bibliographical references.
   ISBN 0-88730-372-2
   1. Conglomerate corporations—Korea (South). 2. Industry and
state—Korea (South). 3. Industrial management—Korea (South).
4. Industrial organization—Korea (South). I. Shin, Yoo Keun.
II. Ungson, Gerardo R. III. Title.
HD2756.2.K8S74 1989
338.8'042—dc20   89-45774
                                           CIP

90 91 92 HC 9 8 7 6 5 4 3 2

Dedicated
with sincere appreciation
to our families

CONTENTS

PREFACE

Recent articles in the popular business press have focused on the impending invasion by Korean companies of the North American marketplace. These articles typically have titles like "The Koreans Are Coming," "Here Comes Korea, Inc.," and so forth, and share a common theme: The United States and Canada are about to see a major increase in imports of Korean products that will further erode the competitiveness of their own products. Parallels with the Japanese experience are drawn, and questions are raised concerning the West's ability to compete or respond effectively to this challenge from the East. There is one problem with articles such as these, however. They are quite incorrect. The Koreans are not coming; they are already here.

Witness, for example, a not atypical American office worker who, after a long day at the office working at his Daewoo Leading Edge microcomputer, drives home in his Hyundai Excel. Once there, he prepares a quick dinner in his Samsung microwave oven and sits down on his Bif sofa to enjoy a quiet evening watching a program on his Goldstar Viewmax combination television/VCR, only to be interrupted by a call on his Korean-made telephone. From home electronics to automobiles to heavy industry, the entrepreneurial skills of Korean companies are gaining a foothold in the global marketplace. How these companies have achieved such prominence out of the ashes of the Korean War is the topic of this book.

Specifically, this book examines the nature of and reasons behind the Korean economic miracle by focusing on the role played by the major Korean corporations, or *chaebols*, in the economic development of the nation. Particular emphasis is placed on Korea's unique approach to management—both from the standpoint of corporate strategy and human resource management. The so-called Miracle on the Han River (referring to the river that runs through Seoul) was made possible by a unique combination of factors, including government policies with respect to industrial development, global market opportunities, the entrepreneurial talents of Korean executives and company founders, and the characteristics of the Korean people themselves. In this book, we focus on two related issues: first, how Korean companies are organized and managed in a way that facilitates their success in the international marketplace; and second, what North Americans can learn from the Korean experience that can enhance their own level of industrial competitiveness. We also look at the role played by cultural differences as they affect management practices and consider some of the serious problems facing Koreans today and threaten their continued economic development. Throughout, we draw comparisons where warranted with comparable situations in Japan and the United States.

In preparing this book, we have been fortunate to have a research team consisting of both Americans and Koreans and to have unusual access to companies and their senior executives, as well as government officials. The two American coauthors made several extended visits to Korea between 1985 and 1988, and the Korean coauthor journeyed to the United States. Data were collected from a variety of independent sources, including archival information, company reports, Korean and U.S. news reports, and business and economic publications in both countries. Our investigation also benefitted from access to Korean publications that were translated into English for our research.

Finally, we secured interviews with approximately 100 managers, executives, scholars, and government officials and conducted interviews in English and, where necessary, in Korean with interpreters. A standardized format was used in these interviews, and the same questions were asked to several individuals (both within and across companies) in order to cross-validate the results. Interview results were also compared with other published sources where possible in order to confirm our understanding of the situation. Every effort was made to verify the accuracy of all information provided to us, but despite these efforts, we realize that errors of translation or simple misunderstandings may have appeared in the final manuscript, for which we assume full responsibility. (It should be noted that in reporting the names of those interviewed, as well as other Koreans, we follow the Asian practice of placing the family name first instead of last.)

This research would not have been possible without the cooperation and support of executives and managers from a wide variety of companies. During the four years of our investigation, we were fortunate to encounter a number of senior executives willing to spend considerable time with us examining both the nature of Korean management practices and the keys to Korea's economic success. Although we cannot in this limited space mention everyone who spoke with us, we would like to acknowledge the valuable assistance of the following individuals. From the chairman's office of Lucky-Goldstar, we thank Executive Director Kim Sang-Bae, Senior Managing Director Kwon Moon-Koo, and Senior Managing Director Kim Yong-Sun, as well as Chairman Hong Sung-Eun and Executive Director Kim Hong Sik from the Lucky-Goldstar Anyang Research Complex and Senior Managing Director Kim Chang Soo of the Goldstar Semiconductor Group. Among those we talked with at Daewoo, we especially thank Executive Vice-President Kim Tae Goo of the Planning and Coordination Division and President Park Sung Kyou of Daewoo Telecom. At Hyundai, special thanks to Vice-President Chung Mong Yoon and to both the former and present directors of the Hyundai Management Training Institute, Shin Myung Cheol and Y. H. Doh.

In addition, we acknowledge Executive Vice-President Park Ung-suh of the International Division of Samsung; Chief Executive Officer Son Kil-Seung of the Office of the Chairman for Management and Planning at Sunkyong; President Park Seong Y. of the Kumho Group; President Park Hyung Koo of Kumho Electric; President Kwon Hyock Jo of Oriental Precision Company; President Chae Hee Kyung of Shinsung Packard; President Huh Seung Hyo of Alto Group; Dr. Lee Yong-Ho, former president of the Seoul Olympic Organizing Committee; Lee Hong Kyu, deputy director of the Industrial Policy Division at the Korean Ministry of Trade and Industry; William E. Franklin, president of Weyerhaeuser Far East, Ltd.; Dr. Richard Walker, Former U.S. Ambassador to Korea; and Kim Wan-Gyoo of the Planning and Controlling Division, Doosan Electro-Materials Company at the Doosan Group.

We also benefitted considerably from discussions with our academic colleagues from several universities. From Korea, these include Former Dean Shim Byung Koo and Professors Kwak Soo-Il, Cho Dong-Sung, Min Sang-Kee, and Park Oh Soo of Seoul National University; Dean Lee Hak-Chong, Park Heung-Soo, and Horace H. Underwood of Yonsei University; and Dean Kim Dong Ki and Professors Hwang Eui-Gak and Kim Linsu of Korea University. From the United States, we acknowledge Professors Edwin A. Miller of the University of Michigan; Jeffrey Pfeffer of Stanford University, William Joyce of Dartmouth College; Robert Doktor of the University of Hawaii; Kae H. Chung of Witchita State University; Mary Ann von Glinow of the University of Southern California; Jay Kim of Ohio State University; Chan Hahn of Bowling Green State University; Song Rhee of Northwest Christian College; G. Cameron Hurst of the University of Kansas; and John Lie and Gerry Fry of the University of Oregon. Finally, we acknowledge a special debt of gratitude to Professor Sang Lee of the University of Nebraska for first providing the two American co-authors with the opportunity to learn about Korea.

During both the research and the writing phases of this project, our work was aided by valuable input from our Korean doctoral students at the University of Oregon. These individuals spent long hours working with us on the project—both in the field and at home—evaluating translations, collecting and verifying data, and providing numerous constructive comments on the manuscript itself as it moved through its various stages. They include Kim Jooyup, Kim Seung Chul, Nan Sanghoon, Park Seung Ho, and Shim Won-Shul, and to them we owe a special debt of gratitude.

This project could not have come to fruition without the patience and support of our families. We express appreciation to Sheila and Kathleen Steers, Hee Sung Shin, and Adad and Luz Ungson for being there when it counted. We also appreciate the support given us by our colleagues both at the University of Oregon and Seoul National University. And our visits to Seoul were made all the more pleasant through the hospitality provided by Min Yong-Shik, senior managing director of the Management and Control Office at Korea Explosives Group, owner of the Seoul Plaza Hotel.

Finally, we acknowledge a special debt to Huh Wan Koo, president of Sungsan Group, for his continued support of our research project as well as for his friendship. People like Mr. Huh serve as exemplary ambassadors for their countries through their patience, thoughtfulness, and generosity to those trying to learn more about cross-cultural differences and industrial competitiveness in a global environment. We are truly indebted for his kindness.

THE CHAEBOL

1 MIRACLE ON THE HAN RIVER

In late summer of 1988 the world turned its attention to Seoul, Korea, and the summer Olympics. Athletes and spectators—and television cameras—from over 160 countries gathered for the event. They witnessed the biggest athletic event of the decade and the coming-out party for a country on the move. Most saw Korea for the first time and were surprised to see not a backward or underdeveloped country reminiscent of old "M∗A∗S∗H" reruns on television, but a nation that was modern, vibrant, forward-looking, and alive with enthusiasm for the future. They saw the modern Korea.

Korea today is a blend of the modern and the traditional. Traditional Korean values are strong and govern most patterns of social interaction, including those of the business world. Yet Korea has also learned much from the West and has incorporated many Western features into its social fabric. As a nation it stresses both personal accomplishment and human relations and places a high value on working for a just cause, whether political freedom or economic development.

THE KOREAN CHALLENGE

From the standpoint of economic development, Korea is a textbook example of success. Since the end of the Korean War, national

1

income has risen over 1,200 percent. South Korea is now the seventeenth-largest economy in the free world and the twelfth-largest trading nation. Its gross domestic product has risen an average of 8.7 percent per year from 1960 to 1988 (*The Economist* 1988a). Last year, exports rose 36 percent, while real growth was 12 percent and unemployment was 2.2 percent. Life expectancy has increased by more than twenty years, and infant mortality has declined by over 50 percent. Over 97 percent of the nation is literate, a figure far exceeding that of most industrialized countries, including the United States.

Korea is developing a significant middle class. In 1970, for example, only 2 percent of the households had refrigerators, only 4 percent had telephones, and 6 percent had televisions. Today, these percentages are 71 percent, 50 percent, and 98 percent, respectively. And only 42 percent of household income is spent on food.

Many factors contributed to Korea's rapid economic development—the "Miracle on the Han River"—but considerable credit must go to the business sector. Its major corporations, called *chaebols*, provided the ideas and strategies, the human resources, and the drive for success that enabled Korea to attain its current level of prosperity. Despite this contribution, it is surprising how little the West actually knows about these companies. Hundreds of books have been written about Japanese companies and the Japanese economic recovery, but almost nothing can be found about Korea, despite its emergence as a major global producer and international competitor. Korean companies are remarkable for their size, diversity, and success. Consider the following examples:

The largest and most productive steel mill in the world is the Pohang Iron and Steel Company, near Ulsan in southeastern Korea.

Hyundai Heavy Industries can build a supertanker to unique specifications in about ten months, whereas the same project in the United States or Western Europe typically takes up to three years and costs significantly more.

Korea was the third country in the world (after the United States and Japan and before Western Europe) to build the 256K DRAM chip and is moving toward producing 1 MB and 4 MB DRAM chips.

The tallest building in Asia is the Daihan Life Insurance Building near downtown Seoul.

Japan's principal competitors for the U.S. and European consumer electronics market are the Korean companies Goldstar and Samsung.

Samsung is soon expected to begin assembling the F-16, the United States' most technologically advanced fighter plane, for the Korean air force.

The popular and inexpensive Leading Edge microcomputer is made in Korea by Daewoo.

Car models sold by Pontiac (LeMans) and Ford (Festiva and Escort GT) are produced in Korea by Daewoo and Kia, and Hyundai will shortly begin assembling cars in Canada for Chrysler for the U.S. market.

The most successful sales record ever set for a new car entry for both the United States and Canada is not made in Japan but is the Hyundai Excel from Korea.

Nine Korean companies are listed among the 1988 International Fortune 500 and four are in the top Fortune 100 among companies outside the United States (*Fortune* 1988). Companies like Hyundai, Daewoo, Samsung, and Goldstar are rapidly becoming household names in the United States and Canada because of their successful marketing of consumer electronics products. Many other Korean companies have grown rapidly by serving as original equipment manufacturers (OEMs) for products sold under U.S. brand names (such as General Electric microwave ovens made by Samsung). Indeed, even the Japanese are impressed with the success of Korean enterprise in the areas of shipbuilding, consumer electronics, computers, and automobiles (B. J. Lee 1988; Sullivan 1988a).

Korean corporations have become world-class players in the international marketplace. Each year they increase their share of world export markets—including the U.S. market—and their presence in industries such as automobiles, household appliances, electronics, and semiconductors is rapidly increasing. How has an almost forgotten underdeveloped nation become a major world economic force in such a short period of time, and what role did Korean corporations play in this process? To discover the answers to these questions, this book explores the nature of Korean corporations and the reasons for their success. It examines government policies that fostered the growth and development of the chaebols and explores how these companies differ from their Japanese and U.S. counterparts. Corporate strategy, management style, work environment, personnel policies, and labor relations are analyzed, as are the major problems and prospects facing these companies and the West as we approach the twenty-first century.

KOREA: THE LAND AND ITS PEOPLE

The way Koreans do business with themselves and others is strongly influenced by their cultural heritage, and without an awareness of this rich history and culture, contemporary observers of the Miracle on the Han River will likely miss key lessons for the future. The remainder of this chapter, therefore, provides a brief overview of Korean geography, history, and culture.

The Republic of Korea (South Korea) occupies the southern half of the Korean peninsula (see Exhibit 1-1). Its only land boundary is with the Democratic People's Republic of Korea to the north. South Korea is approximately 966 kilometers (600 miles) long and 217 kilometers (135 miles) wide and covers a land mass of 99,117 square kilometers (38,925 square miles)—about the size of the state of Indiana. China is to the far north, bordering North Korea, and Japan lies 193 kilometers (120 miles) to the east.

Most of Korea (approximately 80 percent) consists of rugged mountainous terrain that historically has helped Koreans defend themselves from various invasions and preserve traditional culture. At the same time, however, it has hindered both commerce and agriculture: Land suitable for planting is in limited supply, and transportation is difficult although improving.

South Korea today has a population of over 42 million people, approximately 80 percent of whom live in urban areas. Over 10 million people live in Seoul, the capital and commercial and political hub of the country. The next largest cities, Pusan and Taegu, have populations of 3.4 million and 2 million, respectively. As is repeatedly pointed out to visitors, Seoul lies only twenty-eight miles (or "thirty seconds by missile") from the North Korean border—which heightens Koreans' continual awareness of possible security threats from the north.

The Korean people are believed to be descendants of several Mongolian tribal groups that migrated from Manchuria in prehistoric times. These groups eventually became a homogeneous race quite distinct from either the Chinese or the Japanese. The Korean lan-

Exhibit 1-1.   Map of Korea and Neighboring Countries.

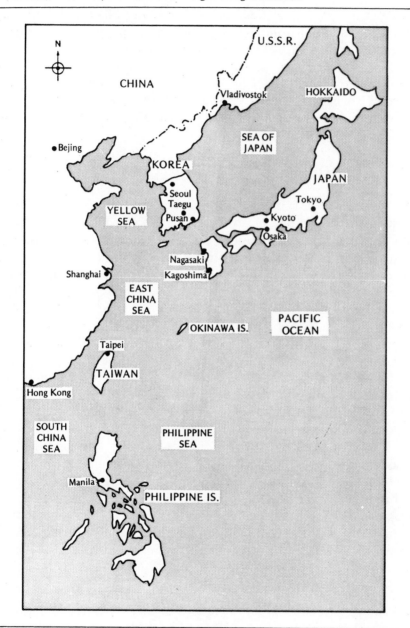

Source: Reprinted by permission from *Fodor's Korea* (New York: Fodor's Travel Publications, A Division of Random House, 1988), p. viii.

guage belongs to the Ural-Altaic family and originally had more in common with Turkish, Finnish, Mongolian, and Hungarian than Chinese. However, over time and as a result of Chinese influence, the language assumed an increasingly Chinese flavor, and until the mid-fifteenth century all Korean writing consisted of Chinese characters. In 1446 King Sejong, perhaps the most revered leader in Korean history, introduced the *han-gul* alphabet to better represent the Korean language sounds—a step that moved Korea and the Koreans closer to the development of a national identity.

HISTORICAL BACKGROUND

The history of Korea is one of struggle and change. After centuries of existing in the shadow of stronger neighbors to the north and east and repelling repeated invasions by the Chinese, the Japanese, the Mongols and others, Korea is still called the Land of the Morning Calm. Its history has been characterized by adaptation and innovation: Koreans have adapted many Chinese customs and have, in turn, passed on many customs to the Japanese. Even so, Korea is neither a miniature China nor Japan: It has retained its own identity and culture.

According to Korean folklore the nation was begun by its mythical founder, Tan'gun. According to legend, Hwanung, the son of the divine creator Hwanin, descended to earth, where he married a bear turned woman and had a son named Tan'gun. Tan'gun welded the various primitive tribes into a single kingdom, which he ruled from 2333 B.C. to 1122 B.C. At this time, Kija, who was supposedly a descendant of the mythical Shang royal line in China, arrived to establish himself as ruler, whereupon Tan'gun resumed his spirit form and returned to the heavens. Archaeological studies demonstrate that people did inhabit the peninsula as early as 4270 B.C., and that around 109 B.C. the Han empire of China conquered what is now Korea, all of which seem to reinforce the myth of Kija, the Chinese invader.

Three Kingdoms Period

During the Han occupation the Chinese tried to integrate Koreans into Chinese society but without much success. After the fall of the

Han dynasty in the first century A.D., one Korean tribal state, the Koguryo, emerged as a tribal alliance of nomadic people in southeastern Manchuria, and two kingdoms emerged in the south—the Paekche and the Silla (also spelled *Shilla*). By the fourth century Koguryo had developed into a sizeable kingdom with a centralized government built around a hereditary military aristocracy, and these three kingdoms dominated the Korean peninsula.

The Silla Dynasty

From 598 to 647 the Chinese launched four major invasions against Koguryo in an effort to gain control in the region. All failed until the T'ang emperor of China allied himself with the king of Silla and attacked Paekche, in preparation for a later attack against Koguryo. By 660 Paekche had been conquered, and by 668 the two allies had conquered Koguryo: The Unified Silla Period had begun. After this victory the Chinese attempted to establish administrative control over all of Korea, thereby challenging the new Silla rulers, and Silla responded by forming an alliance with the defeated Koguryo, ultimately forcing the Chinese out of Korea. This victory in 735 is often referred to as the beginning of Korea as a unified state.

Silla established its capital in Kyongju, near Pusan. Buddhism flourished and was adopted as the official state religion. The magnificent Pulguksa Temple was built as the state Buddhist center, and creative ventures such as the Sokkuram stone cave shrine were completed. Chinese civilization flourished in the region: Art and architecture, the written Chinese language, and Confucian principles of bureaucracy and organization were introduced.

The Silla dynasty was a period of aristocratic supremacy. In this highly stratified hierarchy based on birth, royalty and other aristocracy monopolized all high offices. By the ninth century, however, greed and internal rivalries intensified, and the foundations of the dynasty began to crack. Prominent among the lower echelons who were excluded from power was the increasingly wealthy merchant class, the precursors of the contemporary chaebol families. This unrest led to an insurrection that ultimately caused the downfall of the dynasty and the emergence of a new dynasty starting in 935 under the rule of Wang Kon.

The Koryo Dynasty

The new dynasty, known as the Koryo dynasty, lasted for 450 years and marked further advancement of Korean culture. Among the many important events that characterized this period, three are particularly relevant for an understanding of contemporary corporations in Korea. First, Confucianism began to overtake Buddhism as the preeminent model of correct behavior in society. The new Korean rulers introduced competitive civil service examinations in 958 as a means of filling the highest offices with members of the ruling class who were most competent in Chinese literature and the Confucian classics. Once selected for office, however, advancement depended primarily on social status and seniority. Order, respect, and one's place in an organization became critical determinants of social behavior.

Second, Korea began to develop as a technological and intellectual stronghold. For example, the idea of typography using movable metal type to print multiple copies of one document was invented in Korea in the mid-twelfth century, 200 years before Europeans discovered this technology. Art and religious scholarship also flourished during this period. In short, while many Westerners today may express surprise at Korea's ability to develop competitive technologies, in fact Koreans have done this many times throughout their history.

Finally, the Koryo dynasty is important for an understanding of contemporary Korean-Japanese relations. Toward the end of the fourteenth century, Korea was repeatedly attacked by Japan but by repelling these attacks proved to itself that Japan, although bigger and more powerful, was not invincible—either in war or in commerce. As the Koryo dynasty gave way to the new Yi dynasty in 1392, its contributions to an organized society committed to achievement and success were well established. Perhaps the most potent reminder of this era of achievement is the name for modern Korea: It is derived from the word *Koryo (ko-ree-o)*.

The Yi Dynasty

As is typical with most dynastic shifts, a period of war and rebellion preceded the emergence of the new Yi dynasty. A Mongol invasion and accompanying civil unrest led to the emergence of General Yi Song-gye, who first reestablished order and then proceeded to overthrow the last remnants of the Koryo dynasty and establish his own. The new ruler promptly resumed diplomatic and tributary relations with Ming China and took the ancient Chinese name for Korea—*Choson*, meaning "Land of the Morning Calm."

The Yi dynasty was marked by further cultural and economic development. During the reign of King Sejong in the mid-fifteenth century progressive ideas in administration, linguistics, music, science, and humanistic studies were developed. He established the Hall of Talented Scholars to promote research in institutional traditions, politics, and economics and oversaw the development of new inventions like astronomical and water clocks, rain gauges, and weather forecasting. King Sejong implemented a new Korean alphabet, known as *hangul*. In many areas, Korea was far ahead of European technological developments of the time.

Nevertheless, the Yi dynasty was characterized by consistent warfare. During the 1500s the Japanese initiated a new series of invasions under Hideyoshi Toyotomi. By allying themselves with the Chinese and through several ingenious naval campaigns, Korea again emerged victorious but at great personal and economic cost. Later came war with the Manchus and a brief Chinese occupation in 1636, followed by further political and economic decline.

Finally, beginning in the mid-1800s a new opponent emerged: the West. Hostilities broke out with France after Korea refused to engage in open trade, and similar rebuffs of the Germans and then the Americans followed. In 1866 the American ship *General Sherman* steamed into Korean waters to force the Korean government to open commercial relations. The ship reached Pyongyang with a cargo of European goods, but its presence and concomitant show of force so infuriated the Korean people that the ship was attacked and burned. In 1871 the United States invaded Korea with a small fleet to "make" it open its markets. This fleet was also defeated. Once Korea decided to cease being the "hermit kingdom," however, it began to negotiate bilateral trade treaties—first with America in 1882 and later with Great Britain, Germany, Russia, France, and Japan.

The Japanese Occupation

Toward the end of the nineteenth century Japanese, Chinese, and Russian competition in East Asia led to a series of armed conflicts, and when China and then Russia lost their influence in the region, a period of Japanese supremacy began. During the Russo-Japanese War in 1904 Japanese troops were sent to the Korean peninsula, and by 1905 and the end of the war Japanese control of Korea was widely recognized. In the West many saw the occupation as one that would uplift a backward people who had repeatedly proven their incapacity to defend themselves and build a modern society. As the Japanese grip on Korea tightened, various Korean ministers appealed repeatedly for help from the Western powers but to no avail: The Japanese formally annexed Korea in 1910.

By all accounts, the period of occupation was a cruel one. Japan saw Korea as a colony that could be exploited in support of the Japanese industrial complex. Nevertheless, the Japanese also built highways, railroads, ports, and communications facilities and in doing so created a modern industrial infrastructure for Korea. An elaborate government bureaucracy was also established, albeit one that reported ultimately to Tokyo, and modern schools were built on the Japanese model. In many ways the material well-being of some Koreans improved—but at a cost. As part of the colonization process, efforts were made to eliminate all vestiges of a distinct Korean culture. Laws were passed forbidding all political activities. Books about Korean heros and history were destroyed. Indeed, new books were written in which the history of Korea was reinterpreted with Japan in a favorable light. Finally, the Korean language was essentially outlawed; all teaching, newspapers, and commerce were to be in Japanese. Korean traditional dress was proscribed, and anyone resisting these efforts in any way was punished severely. In short, Japan campaigned to make Korea a "little Japan," although clearly not an equal to Japan.

The Korean War

Japan's repressive rule ended with the close of World War II. At Yalta the Russians and the Western powers decided that Japanese forces above the thirty-eighth parallel would surrender to the Soviet Union, while those south of the parallel would surrender to the Americans. This division of Korea was intended to be temporary but, once created, became a barrier that no amount of negotiation could dissolve. In the north, Kim Il-sung emerged as the leader of

a new People's Republic; in the south the United States first retained some Japanese officials and later established a military government with American personnel as executives and Koreans in subordinate positions.

In 1947 the United Nations General Assembly called for the
creation of a unified and independent government in Korea and
appointed a temporary commission to oversee elections, but when
the Soviets denied access to the northern half of the country, elections were held only in the south. On 10 May 1948, a constituent
assembly was selected to draft a new constitution and elect a new
leader. Shortly thereafter, on 15 August Rhee Sungman was elected
South Korea's first president.

Between December 1948 and June 1949 most Russian and U.S.
troops left Korea. The resulting vacuum and the weak Rhee government created an opportunity for North Korea to invade the South on
25 June 1950. The United States responded by sending troops back
into Korea and shortly thereafter requested and received United
Nations support for such a move. By the end of the war in July 1953
Korea lay in ruins. Hundreds of thousands had died, and millions
were homeless. Moreover, the country's hope of reunification was
more remote than ever. From a commercial standpoint, the budding
industrial base that had developed before the conflict was almost
eliminated.

The Rebuilding

After the war, Korea in many ways was without direction. The Rhee
government seemed preoccupied with solidifying its power through
favoritism and corruption and became increasingly authoritarian.
Following student revolts in 1960, Rhee was forced into exile. This
was followed by a brief democratic experiment under the presidency
of Yun Po-son, with Chang Myon as prime minister. Although committed to democratic principles the Chang government was unable to
maintain itself in power, and in a military coup, in May 1961 Major
General Park Chung-hee assumed control of the government.

Park's authoritarian rule was marked by increasing centralization
of power and a national obsession with economic growth and development. Park's idea of Korean-style democracy emphasized administrative efficiency and the initiation of a series of development pro-

grams to lay the foundation for an economic renaissance for his country. Park was widely criticized for his authoritarian style, but under his direction Korean per capita income rose from $94 in 1960 to $1,589 in 1980 (Steinberg 1989). Exports grew from $33 million to $17 billion during the same period. Life expectancy increased by ten years, and infant mortality was cut in half. Koreans had begun the long march toward economic prosperity.

Following Park's assassination in 1979, Major General Chun Doo Hwan took control. Like Park before him, Chun traded his military uniform for the requisite dark business suit and was given the title of president. The authoritarian rule continued, however, as did the economic prosperity. By 1988 per capita income had risen to around $4,000, annual exports had grown to $60 billion, and annual imports stood at $53 billion (Bank of Korea 1989). Korea had become a major world trading power and a force to be reckoned with by its trading partners, including the United States. Korea's momentum increased to the point that it alarmed several countries. Escalating negative balances of trade led some countries to talk of unfair Korean competition and closed Korean domestic markets; protective legislation was introduced in several legislatures, including the United States.

The Chun government was never a popular one and was marked by intermittent student riots. As Korea approached the 1988 Seoul Olympics—its official coming out party in the global community— the Chun government determined that its political situation should approach its economic status in the world. Following tumultuous negotiations and a chaotic national election, Major General Roh Tae Woo was elected president in what most outside observers considered a relatively fair election. Perhaps the final irony of this election was that opposition candidates, who based their campaigns on charges of antidemocratic governmental behavior, lost the election in large measure because they failed to learn the first lesson of democracy: compromise. The opposition candidates refused to cooperate, thereby splitting the vote and allowing Rho to emerge victorious with only one-third of the popular vote. The new Korea had begun.

BELIEFS AND VALUE SYSTEMS

Research on the social psychology of organizations has established that individual beliefs and value systems are a major influence on managerial behavior. In fact, it has been argued that personal beliefs and values influence such behavior in at least six ways (England 1967). They influence:

A manager's perceptions of the problems and situations to be faced;

A manager's decisions and solutions to problems;

The way managers look at other individuals and groups, thereby influencing interpersonal relationships;

Definitions of personal and organizational success and achievement;

The standards of ethical managerial behavior;

The extent to which managers accept or resist organizational pressures and goals.

If Westerners are to better understand the nature of contemporary Korean corporations and their managements, we need at least a rudimentary understanding of the belief systems and values that form the foundation of Korean culture. The essence of a culture cannot be delineated in a short space, but the following overview of some of the more salient influences on organizational behavior today makes clear that Korean corporations combine traditional values with a unique contemporary outlook that makes them formidable competitors in today's global business environment.

Traditional Values

The traditional foundations of Korean culture trace much of their heritage to Confucianism and neo-Confucian values. Confucius (Kong Fu Ze) was a senior civil servant who lived in China around 500 B.C. Known for his wisdom and insight, Confucius promulgated a code of ethical behavior (not to be confused with a religion) that guided interpersonal relationships in everyday life (Rhee 1985). This code permeates contemporary human relationships in Korean companies and is summed up in the so-called five cardinal virtues:

1. In the relationship between father and son, the son must show love, respect, and absolute obedience to the father. This principle of *filial piety and respect* is inviolate and is the source of the "familism" that permeates Korean society today. The family is vitally important because it defines who people are and where they belong in the larger society. The family looks after its own,

a factor that leads to the nepotism often seen in Korean companies. As a part of this familism, the family emphasizes education and continual self-improvement as a means of aiding the development of self, family, and community. Each individual has an obligation to maximize his or her contribution to the family. For example, as shown in Exhibit 1-2, the average ten- to fifteen-year-olds in Korea spend more time doing homework than even their Japanese counterparts, and the results of these efforts clearly pay off. A recent study by the U.S. National Science Foundation found that 78 percent of the thirteen-year-olds in Korea had mastered intermediate mathematics, whereas only 40 percent of American students had done so (*Register-Guard* 1989, 5A). Educational accomplishment is of paramount importance in a Confucian society.

2. *The wife must be subservient to the husband.* In this sex role differentiation, women are mothers and wives and must obey the male members of the family or society (Y. C. Kim 1976). Women in the workplace typically have lower job status, receive lower pay, and enjoy less job security than their male counterparts.

3. Social order must be arranged according to *strict seniority*, with the young showing respect and obedience to the old and the old assuming responsibility for the well-being and future of the

Exhibit 1-2. Hours Spent Per Day on Homework by Ten- to Fifteen-Year-Old Children.*

Hours per Day Spent on Homework	Country					
	Korea	Japan	United States	Thailand	United Kingdom	France
None	1.0	3.1	5.6	6.6	10.7	3.0
½ hour or less	11.4	13.0	20.4	31.9	23.0	25.3
1–2 hours	35.4	32.9	47.8	39.5	46.5	49.7
2+ hours	51.4	50.6	21.5	22.1	19.3	21.0

*Percentages do not always add up to 100 percent due to missing data.
Source: Based on Hiroko Sugita, "Self-Portrait: The Changing Family" (based on Japan's Prime Minister's Office Youth Policy Board Survey for International Children's Year), *Nippon Steel News* (July–August 1988): 5–8.

young. To this day, seniority is the most important determinant of salary and promotion in most Korean companies.

4. *Mutual trust* between friends and colleagues must be established and maintained in both good times and bad. This trust is seen as the key to all human relationships and a major determinant of cultural solidarity. In fact, maintaining harmonious relationships among close work associates is a never-ending pursuit for most Korean employees at all levels in the organization. Business activity is based more on personal relationships and contacts than on written contracts. Reciprocity and exchange represent an impor-part part of this process.

5. *The absolute loyalty* of the subject to the ruler must be maintained at all times, just as it is between father and son. It is the origin of the strong commitment felt by many employees toward the company. In fact, the president of the company often embodies the essence of the company itself and as such is to be respected and followed without question.

According to the five cardinal virtues, the fundamental nature of human relationships in Korea is not that of interactions among equals but rather interactions among unequals. "Correct" interpersonal behavior is determined by gender, age, and position in society, and a breach in this social etiquette carries severe penalties.

To these Confucian values—indeed, in large part because of them—must be added two further characteristics: *kibun* and face. *Kibun* is a uniquely Korean characteristic that has to do with one's feeling of internal peace and harmony or well-being (Crane 1978). The word has no English equivalent but is similar in meaning to mood. When one's *kibun* is good, everything is at peace; when it is bad, one feels "like eating worms." Because it is vitally important in interpersonal relationships in Korea that one not disturb another individual's *kibun*, great efforts are often made not to convey bad news or news someone does not wish to hear. To a foreigner, this often comes across as deceit—as, for example, when a tailor promises to complete a suit by a certain time when he knows it cannot be done. Rather than being deceitful, the tailor is simply trying to avoid giving the customer bad news, thereby disturbing his *kibun*. This behavior bears a resemblance to the Japanese practice of seldom saying no to any request. One must preserve the internal tranquility of others—especially superiors—at all cost.

In addition, the concept of face is a central tenet of modern Korean society. Face represents the confidence society has in one's moral character (Ho 1976), and without it an individual cannot function properly in the community. Loss of face occurs when an individual, either through personal action or the action of people close to him, fails to meet essential requirements of the social position he occupies. Hence, an individual who cannot keep a commitment—however small—loses face. Similarly, a person who is not treated in accordance with his or her station or position in society loses face. Thus, a senior manager loses face if it becomes known that a junior colleague is earning a higher salary or is promoted ahead of him.

The importance of these two concepts of kibun and face cannot be overestimated. Losing face, for instance, represents a serious threat both to one's position in society and to one's feeling of self-worth and dignity, and suicides are often traced directly to such a loss. As such, all forms of interpersonal interactions in Korean corporations must consider the dynamics of these two characteristics as they relate to work and well-being.

Contemporary Outlook

Traditional values characterize much of Korean life, but they combine in a curious way with contemporary values to affect how business is conducted. Many of these newer values result from the significant changes Korea has had to undergo during the past several decades. The Japanese occupation prior to World War II, for instance, introduced significant changes in the administrative, legal, and educational fields (Rhee 1985), even though the extent of this influence was somewhat limited by the restrictions placed by the Japanese on Korean participation in economic planning and management.

Since World War II and the concomitant increase in Western involvement in Korean affairs after the Korean War, many so-called Western values have increasingly taken hold in Korean society. With increasing urbanization, globalization, and democratization, Koreans are in ever-increasing contact with people from other countries. More and more young people are being educated in the West, particularly the United States, and they tend to take home new ideas to blend with their own. Even for Koreans who never leave the country, the continual presence of the American military is a further influence on social patterns. In fact, Rhee argues that the people of Korea today can be grouped into three categories: the very old, whom he refers to as the Yi-dynasty group; those between ages fifty and seventy, who were influenced by the Japanese occupation; and the younger generation, whose educational background has been influenced by the imported Western ideology of democracy.

The blending of these three traditions has resulted in the emergence of a people who place high value on achievement, individualism (especially compared to the Japanese), perseverance, loyalty, optimism, and a nationalism approaching xenophobia (Hurst 1984; Hofstede, Geert, and Bond 1988). Koreans also have a strong sense of national cohesiveness, due in part to their unitary ancestral roots: They are proud to have maintained a single blood line throughout their 4,000-year history, despite repeated invasions. These traditional values have been reinforced during the period of industrialization. In addition, however, possibly because of repeated invasions and occupations, Koreans appear preoccupied with survival (K. D. Kim 1987). National security and business development are intimately interrelated, and many of the government policies that made possible the growth and development of Korea's major business enterprises were a pragmatic attempt to centralize both effort and limited resources to ensure safe, timely, and predictable returns on investment.

2 INDUSTRIAL POLICY IN KOREA

The origins of the chaebol groups can be traced to efforts by the Korean government to spur economic development after the Korean War. Although many of the companies existed as small enterprises before the war—Doosan, for example, was founded in 1898 and is probably the oldest such group—the drive for economic growth and expansion beginning in the early 1960s created the special circumstances conducive to significant growth and achievement. The Korean government felt that it could best achieve its goal of rapid economic development by identifying target industries—*and target companies*—and providing these industries and companies with the assistance they needed to grow and prosper.

Through a series of five-year plans, Presidents Park and Chun selected companies that were given free reign to produce and export. It was widely believed that concentrating economic power in the hands of a few big family-held enterprises represented a cost-efficient and expeditious path to development. Chairmen of the companies were held personally accountable to the government for task accomplishment, and the cost of failure was high. The government cleared roadblocks to corporate growth and often provided monopolistic conditions (and resulting economies of scale) that were conducive to success. Even so, achieving the government's objectives would have been impossible without the entrepreneurial talents of the company founders and the dedication of employees who labored long hours at low pay to help the companies meet their objectives. Traditional Korean culture combined with a pragmatic contemporary outlook to pave the way to success. A case in point is the Samsung Group.

In his autobiography, published shortly before his death in 1987, Lee Byung-Chull, founder and chairman of Korea's largest company, describes the many obstacles he struggled against in his quest to build a major enterprise. Founded in 1938 with a total capital of $2,000 (U.S.) and forty employees, Samsung (meaning "three stars" in Korean) Company was enjoying limited growth as a small trading company when the 1950 Communist invasion into the south forced Lee to abandon his major operations in Seoul. His inventories were stolen (by soldiers and politicians on both sides of the conflict, according to Lee), and he was left with almost nothing. Retreating back to Taegu, where the company was originally founded, Lee met with the manager and staff of his last remaining enterprise, Choson Brewery. When he told of his plight, the manager replied simply, "Mr. President, there is nothing to worry about. We have some savings, and with these funds you can start the new business that you want" (B. C. Lee 1987, 39). Moving to Pusan in 1951, Lee used the funds to create Samsung Trading Co., Ltd., and within one year corporate assets had increased twentyfold.

The company continued to prosper as it moved increasingly into manufacturing. By 1965 fertilizer was in short supply and high demand as Korea's agricultural sector expanded, and Lee determined that his next project would be to build the largest fertilizer company in the world. With loans of $42 million and licensed technology and technical assistance from Mitsui of Japan, he received government approval for the project and selected Ulsan as a building site. Many people—including many business leaders—felt the business venture was too risky to succeed. After all, how could "little Korea" attempt such a major enterprise? Lee personally selected the project manager, who for the next eighteen months slept and ate with the construction crews, leaving his family at home.

When construction was nearly 80 percent completed, Samsung was charged with an illegal sale of about $50,000 worth of goods. While the company argued that the sale had been a clerical oversight, the government (and government-controlled newspapers) continued to create a scandal and arrested Lee's second son. Much later it was brought out that Lee had been approached before the scandal by a high-ranking politician who asked for—but did not receive—a "donation" of 30 percent of Korea Fertilizer's stock. The scandal continued until Lee agreed to a proposal to complete the fertilizer plant at his own expense and donate the facility to the government. With this, the scandal dissolved and his son was released from jail.

At about the same time Lee also decided to enter the mass communication business. As he tells it, "I consulted with [Korean] President Park about this, and he gave his consent on the spot. Immediately, he telephoned Mr. Hong Jong-Chull, the Minister of Culture and Information, and directed him to support me positively on this project. Thus, Radio Seoul began its broadcast" (B. C. Lee 1987, 50). Shortly thereafter, a television station, Tongyang Television Broadcasting Corporation (TTBC), was added, followed later by a daily newspaper, the *Joong-ang Daily News.* Using the credo, "the best facilities, the best treatment, and the best people produce the best quality goods," all three ventures proved to be highly successful.

The editorial policies of these businesses, however, were not always to the government's liking. Although Lee's telecasts and publications did not confront the government directly, they stressed the enhancement of morality, a message not lost on many people. Shortly after President Park was assassinated and President Chun took control, the government declared that all private television stations would be merged into the government-owned Korean Broadcasting System. TTBC and the new ten-story building Lee had just completed were turned over to the government on 30 November 1980.

Thus, Lee experienced three major setbacks and major financial losses yet he recovered and with a loyal cadre of employees made Samsung bigger and stronger than it was before. Today, Samsung is ranked as the thirty-second–largest company in the world in sales and the twentieth largest outside the United States (*Fortune* 1988), and it shows no signs of slowing down.

In many ways, the story of Lee Byung-Chull and Samsung is not unique for Korea. Indeed, this story illustrates the fairly typical pattern of growth and development of companies such as Lucky-Goldstar, Daewoo, Hyundai, and others: the dedication and achievement of Korean entrepreneurs and workers as well as the supportive government policies and close business-government relationships that helped create conditions for growth. Because of a unique set of circumstances that were present in Korea, stories like Samsung's also provide evidence that in many ways Korean companies are distinct from most companies in the West. This chapter explores the origins of Korea's major corporations and the government policies that facilitated their growth and development.

GENERAL APPROACHES TO INDUSTRIAL POLICY

To understand the success of companies like Samsung, it is helpful to first examine the government policies that facilitated their growth and development. This discussion explores the reasons behind industrial planning on a national level and reviews the nature of the relationship between business and government over the past three decades. Indeed, this close relationship has led some observers to refer to the business-government establishment as "Korea, Inc."

By any standards, Korea's ascendancy as a world-ranked competitor has been astonishing. In 1965 Korea's GNP per capita was $100; by 1988 this figure had increased to over $4,000. Its economy grew twentyfold during the 1965–85 period—a feat accomplished by Japan about fifteen years earlier. Korea's growth rate has been remarkable, averaging almost 9 percent per annum over this twenty-year period. Exports grew by over 100 percent from 1980 to 1986 alone, compared to 62 percent for Japan and a negative 2 percent for the United States during the same period (*Newsweek* 1988).

Korea's economic development can also be understood in terms of its changing trade profile. In 1970 its top five exports were textiles and garments, plywood, wigs, minerals, and electronic products. In 1985 the top five exports were listed as textiles and garments, ships, electronic products, steel products, and footwear. Although textiles and garments still constitute the largest source of foreign exchange, some light manufacturing products are being displaced by more capital-intensive products such as ships, electronic products, and steel. These changes in the composition of Korea's exports reflect shifts in industrial policies aimed at enhancing Korea's competitiveness in the world market.

The Structure of Industrial Policy

Industrial policy can mean many different things—from a plan to aid particular industries with subsidies, tariffs, and tax breaks to more centralized planning that identifies growth areas for development. Such policies can be distinguished in terms of their degree of governmental intervention and the objectives underlying this intervention (see Exhibit 2–1).

At the extreme ends of the spectrum are laissez-faire competition and centralized planning. The principle underlying laissez-faire competition is that every individual, if left alone to pursue individual needs, achieves the best results for all. Except for the brief period in the nineteenth-century when the United States and Great Britain were primarily agricultural states, there have not been many contexts for laissez-faire or for a truly free market. At the other extreme is centralized planning, as exemplified in the Soviet Union or China (until the recent past), in which the government engages in the total planning for the economy. Other forms of intervention, such as socialism in selected parts of Europe or "administrative guidance" in Japan, fall between these two ends.

In spite of U.S. predilections for a free-market system, the most common practice around the world is one of government intervention. In fact, one can argue that all governments intervene in the private sector; their only difference is the underlying purpose for intervention. The United States intervenes mainly for purposes of regulation (Neuberger 1983). This is typified best by antitrust legislation and the Federal Trade Commission's veto power over mergers. Both represent interventions that regulate or police competitive activity rather than develop it. Japanese government interventions, however, focus more on developing the national economy and recognize the need to shape competitive activity so that development in a particular direction will occur (Johnson 1984).

European industrial policies are interventionist in form but differ substantively from the content of Japanese policies. In the case of West Germany and France, for example, intervention is made on behalf of "national champions," but only after a period of competition. In contrast to the Japanese practice, "national champions" in West Germany and France do not engage in fierce competition after their selection.

Types of Industrial Policies

In conjunction with overall development, industrial policies serve a country's need to catch up, stay ahead, or "leap-frog" over world

Exhibit 2-1. Patterns of Business-Government Relationships.

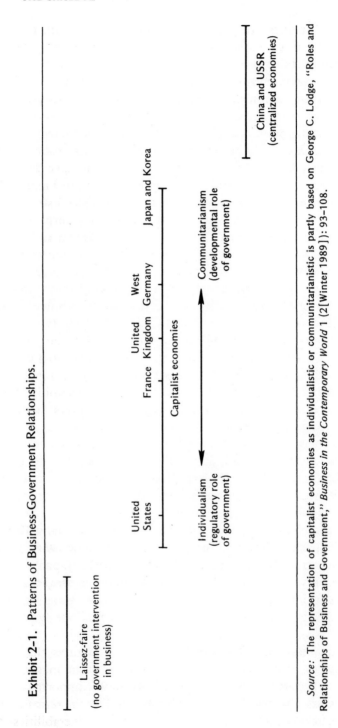

Laissez-faire
(no government intervention
in business)

United
States

France

United
Kingdom

West
Germany

Japan and Korea

Capitalist economies

Individualism
(regulatory role
of government)

Communitarianism
(developmental role
of government)

China and USSR
(centralized economies)

Source: The representation of capitalist economies as individualistic or communitarianistic is partly based on George C. Lodge, "Roles and Relationships of Business and Government," *Business in the Contemporary World* 1 (2[Winter 1989]): 93–108.

competitors. At different times, many countries have practiced various types of industrial policy. *Defensive industrial policies* preserve existing structures, maintain employment, and protect beleaguered industries. Import quotas, used in the case of automobiles by the U.S. and European firms against Japanese products, is an example of a defensive industrial policy.

On the other hand, *adaptive industrial policies* encourage and facilitate industrial change by providing resources from aging or declining sectors to more productive sectors. The specification of "sunset" and "sunrise" industries, as practiced by the Japanese and Korean governments, is an example of an adaptive industrial policy. Japanese business-government relationships are frequently presented in terms a pluralistic arrangement in which government and business are engaged in power struggles and "turf wars" among themselves but cooperate with each other where their goals coincide. Government, through the use of policy instruments, "indicates" its preferences through noncoercive methods. Such indications, however, must be formulated in light of the private sector's ability to thwart them. Private industry is free to act on its own, but if it chooses to go against governmental wishes, it does so at the potential loss of special governmental consideration. A good example of this in Japan can be seen in the case of Honda, which entered the automobile market (quite successfully) despite the opposition of Japan's Ministry of International Trade and Industry.

EVOLUTION OF INDUSTRIAL POLICY IN KOREA

Although the comparison is not readily accepted by many Koreans, the prevailing belief internationally is that Korea, along with Taiwan, Hong Kong, and Singapore, resembles a "little" Japan. That is, Korea's success is facilitated by imitating Japan's strategies and economic institutions. Neither the Japanese, Korea's former colonizer, nor the Koreans, who resent the colonization period, are sympathetic to this analysis.

Yet many economic institutions and infrastructures that led to Japan's success—such as the role of government in managing the economy—are mirrored in Korea's development. Important differences between the two countries also exist—both in terms of hierarchical relations and economic and political vulnerabilities—that can lead to variations in policymaking and overall impact on economic development. A review of the relationship between government and business in Korea, as it evolved in both formal and informal industrial policies, helps explain the existence of many of the prominent features of the Korean economy, the relative success of Korean corporations, and the government's present policies.

Korean industrial policy can be classified into three evolutionary stages: (1) the "take-off" period from 1961–73, (2) the shift from general export promotion to sectoral policy from 1973–79, and (3) trade and financial liberalization, started in 1979 and extending to the present time.

The Take-Off Period: 1961–73

Since the postwar period Korea has consistently oriented itself toward aggressive export policies and rapid industrialization. Following the downfall of the Rhee government in 1960, a new policy was enacted that promoted the inflow of foreign resources of all types and the development of Korea's exports. The take-off phase featured wide-ranging interventions in export promotion, industry finance, and protectionism.

During this period, several key reforms were instituted, including (1) fiscal and monetary policies aimed at increasing public and private saving, (2) a uniform exchange rate, and (3) a free trade zone in 1970. The success of these policies is partly manifested in the spectacular growth in the value of Korea's exports from $50 million in 1962 to $25 billion in 1982. Companies like Samsung (discussed previously) benefited considerably from these policies.

Also at this time, the government focused considerable attention and resources on developing a suitable industrial infrastructure. A good example of this can be seen in the Pohang Iron and Steel Company (referred to in Korea as POSCO). Begun in 1968 by the Korean government, POSCO's goal was to establish Korea as a major steel producer and competitor in the world market. In addition, POSCO was designed to provide much-needed inputs for Korea's manufacturing sector. POSCO's first plant was built near Ulsan, and in the early 1980s, due to the success of this facility, a second major plant was built in Kwangyang.

By any standard of comparison, POSCO has been a success. Not only has the venture been profitable—no easy task in the steel indus-

Exhibit 2-2. Comparison of 1988 Steel Prices by Country.

Country	Steel Products ($ per ton)		
	Hot Coil	Plate	Cold Rolled Coil
Korea	$320	$326	$451
Taiwan	385	385	473
Japan	638	688	765
United States	435	491	621

Source: Data based on information supplied by Shim Sung Won, "Pohang Iron and Steel Company: The Days of the Steel Giant," Business Korea, April 1988, 51.

try—but it also has become the largest such venture in the world, with total 1987 sales of 10,916,000 tons and a net profit after taxes of approximately $85 million. As can be seen in Exhibit 2-2, one of the keys to this success is POSCO's ability to produce high-quality steel and sell it on the world market at attractive prices. In this way, POSCO has emerged as a symbol of national pride.

Sectoral Policy: 1973–79

Following the general export promotion phase, a new period began featuring more typical sector-oriented import substitution initiatives. The impetus behind this movement was the desire to accelerate changes in Korean comparative advantage, and attention was directed at supporting large-scale, capital-intensive industries. This selection was formalized in five-year economic plans that outlined the direction the government expected the economy to be headed toward, the industries that were "strategic" to this direction, and the industries that were not.

Special incentives were granted to these strategic industries, such as tax exemptions, custom rebates, access to foreign exchange, and other forms of protection or enhancements that allowed these industries to be competitive at a world level. Credit at very low interest rates was provided by the Korea Development Bank, the Korea Exchange Bank, and other government-controlled commercial banks. Informally, considerable pressure was placed on industries, including occasional visits from the president, to comply with governmental directives and meeting or exceeding production targets.

The success of governmental initiatives in the private sector can be explained by the lack of capital, or access to capital, in Korea during its early developmental period (Woronoff 1986). This made Korean businesses dependent on the government for financial assistance and provided the government with leverage in implementing its export goals. Another reason was Korea's shortage of skilled entrepreneurs. Because Japan had dominated commercial enterprise and had used its own people to staff its industries, Koreans did not have many opportunities to develop their talents. Hence, Korea's selection policy was based on the government's desire to quickly fill the entrepreneurial gap by supporting those who were most promising.

The policy of selecting and supporting particular individuals and their companies who were considered loyal and reliable led to the formation of large business groups, the chaebols. Coming into prominence in the 1970s, the chaebols have been Korea's leading agents of the export of capital goods and related services. These chaebol groups have spurred growth in a variety of basic and advanced industries, such as steel, shipbuilding, consumer electronics, petrochemicals, and industrial construction. A good example here is Hyosung Group, Korea's seventh-largest corporation. Founded in 1957, Hyosung expanded significantly in the 1970s as a result of prevailing government policies and branched into manufacturing, apparels, batteries, aluminum, metal products, construction, and real estate. Today, Hyosung has annual sales close to $4 billion.

Trade Liberalization Policy: 1979 and Onward

Korea faced enormous problems at the start of 1979. There was mounting criticism that the sectoral policy was overly ambitious and had led to serious misallocation of resources. In addition, a second oil shock had led to a worldwide recession and the assassination of President Park had created great political uncertainty. Accordingly, Korea embarked on a more cautious path to liberalization in 1979.

The Korean government recognized the importance of indicative planning and the role of the market, which led to a number of financial and trade liberalization policies. First, the government began reversing its past preferences for large, heavy-industry firms in favor of smaller and medium-sized firms. This trend is particularly evident after 1986. Second, it terminated its role in specific credit allocation decisions, forcing companies to rely more on stock offerings and borrowing on the open market. This policy also has been intensified in the past several years. The goal of these policies, when taken together, was to reduce government intervention and open up the market to greater competition—especially for smaller and medium-sized firms. Government and industry were moving farther apart.

Other governmental measures at this time included selling commercial banks to private shareholders, establishing new financial institutions, increasing interest rates to borrowers, and enacting liberalized trade control measures. Again, the movement was toward less government control.

KEYS TO THE SUCCESS OF KOREA'S INDUSTRIAL POLICY

The industrial policies of Korea have proven to be successful. Under them, as noted above, the economic growth rate and industrial development have soared and the country as a whole prospered. Several key factors contributed to this success, including (1) centralized credit policies, (2) supportive organizing structures, (3) supportive infrastructures, (4) a disciplined workforce, and (5) supportive corporate strategies.

Centralized Credit Policies

To a large extent, the success of Korea's industrial policy is anchored on its supportive institutions. Rhee, Ross-Larson, and Pursell (1984) have presented a number of reasons why the Korean government was able to control the actions of the private sector, particularly during the "take-off" stage and the ensuring period of sectoral intervention. First, the government was a major stockholder in domestic banks and had the power to appoint bank managers. Second, it controlled the inflow of foreign capital that was the principal source of corporate loans in Korea. Third, through the Bank of Korea and the Ministry of Finance, it controlled the interest rates in the formal banking sector. This rationing of bank loans provided the government considerable leverage in promoting its export-growth policies. If companies pursued policies the government supported, credit became available; if not, credit dried up.

Supportive Organizing Structures

Another policy mechanism undertaken by the government included the system of setting export targets and the practice of holding monthly national trade promotion meetings that were attended by Korea's president, economic ministers, and leading businessmen. These sessions provided the principal forum in which the various parties could informally negotiate product-mixes and level of administrative incentives. Corporate directions were established and approved at the highest levels of government.

In most developing countries, effective policymaking is facilitated by a strong and competent economic staff, such as that of Japan's Ministry of International Trade and Industry. In Korea, this task was assumed by the Economic Planning Board (EPB), whose minister was also the deputy prime minister of Korea and was accountable to the president (Woronoff 1986). The EPB was entrusted with special powers and responsibilities, such as developmental planning, budgeting, foreign cooperation and investment promotion, and preparing five-year economic plans. To ensure success, these plans were always backed up with solid budgets and financing from various ministries. In order to enhance the probability of success, the career advancement of many higher-level bureaucrats was linked directly to program accomplishment.

Supportive Infrastructures

The government also took an active role in developing and supporting these ministries. Infrastructural development was furthered with the establishment of twenty special corporations that included housing and highway agencies, telecommunications authorities, tourism and trade-promotion agencies, and banks. This infrastructure paved the way for economic programs that were enacted later. Historically, business-government relations have been cooperative in nature. High-level business and trade associations have been instrumental in directing and monitoring the implementation of past governmental policies.

Firms and institutions have become successful by working together for mutual benefit.

Debates continue about the wisdom of favoring a few individuals or groups as opposed to a balanced distribution of power and resources. Even so, it is generally agreed that chaebol groups have been instrumental in spurring the growth and development of the Korean economy. Unlike family-based companies in other countries such as Argentina or the Philippines, the founders of chaebols have channeled back profits and resources back into the company and not diverted such funds to unrelated overseas investments. This might explain why Korea succeeded in this type of interfirm grouping and other countries did not.

A Disciplined Workforce

Clearly, a key to Korea's success in its export policy is its low wage rates compared to those of its competitors. Beyond these comparisons, however, much can be said about Korean management in general and the tenacity of Korean workers in particular. Examples abound of Korean men and women who labor passionately in factories, hoping that their sacrifices will lead to better lives for their sons and daughters.

Can the Korean management system make a difference in international competition? Clearly, Korea's labor costs of approximately two dollars an hour or less have made a lasting impression on competitors, particularly the Japanese, who feel pressured to accelerate their timetable for exiting from the steel, shipbuilding, and heavy machinery industries. Less evident, perhaps, is the discipline and relative social harmony that characterize the Korean workforce. Although not easily documented, such characteristics have a positive impact on the quality of Korean products, and help make them competitive on the world market. We return the characteristics of the Korean workforce in Chapter 6.

Supportive Corporate Strategies

It is now commonly acknowledged that Japanese institutions and economic infrastructures have facilitated Japan's strategies of entering world markets at the low end and systematically gaining market share at the higher ends of the market (Abegglen and Stalk 1985). Korea resembles Japan in this regard. Through indicative planning and mechanisms to ensure compliance, the Korean government effectively steers its economy in proposed directions. The chaebols, though criticized for political favoritism and uncontrolled expansion, function as a clearing house for Korean products in the world market. Like the major corporations in Japan, the chaebols have the necessary size to achieve economies of scale and the scope to compete in the world marketplace. Finally, the Korean workforce provides both the tenacity (in its disciplined workers) and the financial capability (through low labor costs) that enhance a low-cost leadership strategy (see Chapter 5).

Overall, then, several factors came together to facilitate the Miracle on the Han River. Government, management, and labor joined together to bring Korea out of the devastation of the war years and into a period of continued growth and relative prosperity. In fact, Korea has recovered from almost total devastation and become an economic power to be reckoned with—at a rate almost twice as fast as Japan's recovery. And, as many Koreans will tell you, this is only the beginning.

3 CHARACTERISTICS OF KOREAN CORPORATIONS

One of the first sights visitors see on arriving in Singapore is the impressive Raffles City Complex. Designed by American architect I. M. Pei, Raffles City is the largest building project in Asia and includes the tallest hotel in the world, the seventy-three-story Westin Stamford Hotel. The complex also includes two twenty-eight-story towers and a convention center for 5,000. When it was completed in 1985—three months ahead of schedule—it was praised by *Engineering News Record* as an "engineering miracle" (Lie 1988). What often goes unnoticed or unmentioned in discussions about this complex is that this "miracle" was constructed by the Ssangyong Group, Korea's sixth-largest company.

Indeed, this is not the only mammoth construction project successfully completed by Ssangyong in recent years. The company also constructed the Plaza Indonesia (the largest building complex in Indonesia), the Omariya Riyadh office complex in Saudia Arabia, the Al-Shaheed Faisal College and the Shamaishani Center in Jordan, and the Maghreb highway in Kuwait. Moreover, giant construction projects are only one of nineteen businesses managed by the Ssangyong Group, which accrued $4.7 billion in sales in 1987 and had total assets of $4.9 billion. In addition to construction, the group is involved in oil refining, cement production, engine manufacturing, truck and bus manufacturing, shipping, textiles, paper products, electronics, securities, insurance, leisure industries, and international

33

trading—all of which emerged from a humble soap company founded in 1939 by Kim Sung-kon.

Since 1975 Ssangyong (Korean for "twin dragons," symbolizing peace and progress) has been run by the founder's son, Kim Suk Won. Under Kim's guidance, the company's gross sales increased twenty-nine-fold from 1975 to 1987, while total assets increased twenty-three-fold. Ssangyong's strategy is one of diversification, remaining flexible, and changing as Korea and the world economy changes. Its motto—"Integrity, reliability, and creativity"—symbolizes its long-term drive for success. Indeed, the Group's theme is often described as "Let's create one hundred years of history." Chairman Kim often tells his employees, "Let's try to publish a book [entitled] *Ssangyong: 100 Years.* For that we need to build a firm foundation. Ssangyong will always be in Korea no matter who is running the company" (Lie 1988: 497).

If we look closely at Ssangyong, several interesting features emerge. The company is largely family-held, family-managed, and paternalistic. It is characterized by strong centralized planning and control and exhibits a strong entrepreneurial spirit. In order to succeed, the company has pursued a strategy of growth and diversification that is consistent with Korea's economic development goals. Similar characteristics can be found repeatedly across a broad spectrum of Korean companies. This chapter explores the nature of these similarities (as well as some differences) in an effort to discover what makes Korean corporations both unique and successful in global competition. Several distinctive features of chaebol groups are identified, followed by a comparison of these groups with their Japanese counterparts. First, however, we explore more fully the meaning of the term *chaebol.*

DEFINING CHAEBOL

As noted in Chapter 1, the major Korean firms are generally referred to as chaebols. A *chaebol* can be defined as "a business group consisting of large companies which are owned and managed by family members or relatives in many diversified business areas" (Yoo and Lee 1987: 97). In other words, it is a financial clique consisting of varied corporate enterprises engaged in diverse businesses and typically owned and controlled by one or two interrelated family groups. Hyundai, for example, is largely owned and managed by the Chung family under Chung Ju-Yung, while Samsung is largely owned and controlled by the family of its late founder, Lee Byung-Chull. Lucky-Goldstar is largely controlled by the two interrelated Koo and Huh families.

Today, there are over fifty chaebol groups of varying sizes in Korea. The ten largest are shown in Exhibit 3-1, along with their major product lines, annual sales, and number of employees. When examining this list, the reader should recognize that names are sometimes deceiving or at least confusing. For example, although Lucky-Goldstar is in one sense like two companies—its chemicals and cosmetics are manufactured and sold under the "Lucky" label, while its electronics products use the name "Goldstar"—it is a highly integrated if diversified company. Ssangyong Group (the sixth-largest firm in Korea) is often confused with Sunkyong Group (the fifth-largest). But perhaps most confusing is the Korea Explosives Group, the eighth-largest company in Korea. Under the leadership of Chairman Kim Seung Youn, this $4 billion group is involved in a wide variety of enterprises, including energy and petrochemicals, electronics, construction, insurance and securities, transportation, foodstuffs, hotels, and general trading. It also makes explosives.

It is worth noting that for some Koreans the term *chaebol* has the same negative connotations that are often associated with the terms *zaibatsu* in Japan and *conglomerate* in the United States. These negative attributions have resulted in large part from the perception that some of the chaebols accumulated their wealth either because of unfair advantage or government connections. Some but certainly not all of these corporate groupings have been accused of exploiting their employees for the sake of corporate profits. It should be noted, however, that most large-scale enterprises around the world—in the United States, Japan, Western Europe, and even the Soviet Union—have been similarly accused. Despite these accusations, several major Korean companies, such as Lucky-Goldstar and Sunkyong, have received widespread recognition for their positive approach and contributions to employee welfare and community development. This study does not evaluate corporate social responsibility, either in Korea or elsewhere. Rather, it focuses on explaining how the chaebols evolved and developed and on what makes them unique competitors in the international marketplace. In this sense, the term is used simply to mean a closely held, integrated, yet diversified corporate entity that produces a wide array of product lines for global consumption.

Exhibit 3-1. Korea's Ten Largest Corporations (1987 sales).

Rank	Company	1987 Sales (in $ billions)	Number of Employees	Major Products
1	Samsung	$24.0	160,596	Electronics, textiles food processing, insurance
2	Hyundai	22.7	142,630	Autos, industrial machinery, ship-building
3	Lucky-Goldstar	16.0	88,403	Electronic and chemical products
4	Daewoo	16.0	120,000	Computer products, autos, financial services, shipbuilding
5	Sunkyong	7.3	17,985	Video and audio tapes, textiles, petroleum
6	Ssangyong	4.8	16,870	Cement, autos, petroleum
7	Hyosung	3.9	24,000	Heavy industry, textile and building materials
8	Korea Explosives	3.9	18,291	Explosives, agricultural products, industrial machinery
9	Hanjin	3.3	26,683	Transportation, construction, financial services
10	Kia	2.4	23,733	Cars, trucks, machine tools

Source: Ranking and sales figures are from Prudential-Bache and Co. reports as summarized in "Samsung: South Korea Marches To a Different Drummer," *Forbes*, 16 March, 1988, 84–89; Number of employees are from company reports and "The Fortune International 500," *Fortune*, 1 August 1988, D1–D36.

DISTINCTIVE FEATURES
OF THE CHAEBOLS

In some ways, the typical chaebol is similar to the prewar Japanese zaibatsu—indeed, they share the same Chinese characters when written—but they also have major differences. Among the more salient characteristics of the typical chaebol are (1) family control and management, (2) paternalistic leadership, (3) centralized planning and coordination, (4) an entrepreneurial orientation, (5) close business-government relations, and (6) strong school ties in hiring policies.

Family Control and Management

Unlike their Japanese counterparts, most Korean companies are controlled by families through stock ownership. At Hyundai sixteen of the twenty-four companies that comprise the group are at least 50 percent owned by the founder and his family or by other companies controlled by the founder. Of the remaining eight companies, four have about 50 percent of their stock owned exclusively by the Chung family (Matsumoto 1986). A review of the other major companies reveals similar patterns of ownership and control.

This finding is not surprising in view of the relatively short history of the chaebols and in view of the Korean tradition of family responsibility (that is, eldest sons inherit most family property and responsibility). However, in addition to family ownership, there also is active family participation in the management of the companies. Despite the recent trend toward recruiting more executives from outside the family, "management by family" remains a strong tradition. For example, one study found that of the top twenty chaebols, 31 percent of the executive officers were family members, while 40 percent of the executives were recruited from outside the corporation and 29 percent were promoted from within (Yoo and Lee 1987).

A second study by Shin (1985) found that 26 percent of the presidents of the major companies were founders, while 19 percent were the sons of the founders, 21 percent were promoted from within, and 35 percent were recruited from outside. It was noted that although more than 50 percent of the CEOs were not family members, the core managerial positions in nearly all the companies belonged to family members. These findings contrast sharply with comparable Japanese companies in at least two ways. Not only are far fewer executives in Japan family members, but far fewer executives in Japan are chosen from outside the corporation (approximately 8 percent in Japan compared to 35 percent in Korea—see Hattori 1986).

A final study of the centrality of family members in management was done at Lucky-Goldstar (Hattori 1986). This study looked at both the number of family members in each of the companies of the group and assigned weights to each executive to reflect his power or influence in the company. The results indicate that the absolute number of family members per company may be small but the power of these members is quite strong. Hence, one characteristic of the majority of these corporations is the position of dominance held by the various family members: They typically hold both the financial and managerial reins of the company.

Paternalistic Leadership

A second feature of most chaebols is that they are managed by one central, paternalistic figure. The CEO, often the founder, typically assumes personal responsibility for the performance of every aspect of the firm and, as such, feels a responsibility to centralize decision-making and authority to ensure tight controls. Moreover, such a leader usually assumes a personal interest in the welfare and development of those under him. Like the role of the family discussed above, this facet of Korean management follows naturally from the Confucian values of the society: The CEO is a quasi-father figure and as such is to be obeyed in all matters.

The CEO as quasi-father figure is exemplified by Chung Ju-Yung, founder and until recently chairman of the Hyundai Group. At Hyundai, Chairman Chung wielded absolute authority and was known for making all important decisions; no one dared oppose him. Ruling by example, Chairman Chung set aside thirty minutes every morning between 6:00 and 6:30 to receive telephone calls from overseas branches. It has been said that all overseas business operations were directed from his home early each morning. This degree of centralized control over various international divisions is indeed rare in Western—and even Japanese—companies, but centralization of power and authority is particularly noteworthy in groups still managed by the founders. Even so, most Korean presidents of the various companies within one group have very little power compared to their international equivalents, as evidenced by the ease and frequency with which chairmen move personnel around within and across the various group companies.

In fact, a Korean newspaper, *Dong A Ilbo* (1984), described the relationship between the chairman of a chaebol group and his various company presidents as follows: "The meeting of group presidents often serves to impress on the presidents that the distance between them and the group chairman is as great as the distance between them and new recruits. . . . And they all, even those who are formerly ranking government officials or comrades of the founding group chairman, must stand at attention when the group chairman enters the meeting room, even though he may be only in his thirties."

In most chaebols, the chairman meets regularly with his group of presidents. For example, at Hyundai, the chairman meets every Monday and Friday morning with the forty or so presidents. The chairman calls on each president by name, asks a series of questions concerning corporate activities, and settles pressing issues on the spot. At Daewoo, the group presidents' meeting is attended by the chairman, two deputy chairmen, and about ten presidents in charge of relatively important business fields, such as foreign trade, construction, shipbuilding, electronics, automobiles, and so forth. And at Lucky-Goldstar, the Management Committee consisting of eight members of the owner families of Koo and Huh and the president in charge of planning and coordination meet regularly to make the primary decisions. This "presidents' group" emerges as a central vehicle by which the group chairmen discuss corporate activities and issue directives to the various entities regarding present and future activities of the company. Throughout this process, however, the role of the chairman is paramount.

Centralized Planning and Coordination

Partly because of the nature of family-based management and strong authoritarian leadership, the third characteristic of most Korean corporations is the existence of a central planning function that works closely with the group chairmen in reaching decisions and developing strategic plans for future corporate actions. This function also effectively coordinates resource allocation across the various enterprises so that highly complex ventures typically meet with success.

Most chaebols have a planning group, known variously as the Planning and Coordination Office, the Integrated Planning Office, or the Office of the Secretary. The size of this group varies considerably: Hyundai's group consists of approximately 40 managers, while Samsung's over 200. Typically, the planning group resides organizationally in the nucleus company, such as Hyundai Construction Co., and as such often appears to be an organ of that particular company instead of the chaebol as a whole. The cost of maintaining the planning group is apportioned to all companies in the chaebol, and the planning group is typically headed by its own president. Senior members of the office staff often carry the title of senior managing director or managing director.

The primary function of the planning group is to collect, analyze, and present useful information to the chairman for future decision-making. Typically, each member company explains to the president of the planning group what it has accomplished and what it plans to do. This information is then organized and passed onto the chairman prior to the next presidents' meeting. At this meeting, the chairman can ask questions of the various presidents from a position of current (and hopefully accurate) knowledge, and relevant decisions can be made.

In addition, other responsibilities typically assigned to the planning office include conducting regular and unscheduled visits to all companies, planning new business ventures, formulating group strategy, and conducting public relations, advertising, and legal activities on behalf of the whole group. All these activities are conducted under the close scrutiny of the chairman.

Finally, the planning group often plays a major role in personnel decisions. At Hyundai, for example, the Personnel Affairs Committee is chaired by the president of the Planning and Coordination Office. This committee is responsible for screening, hiring, and assigning all new college graduates hired by the company, thereby ensuring continuity and quality across the various units. Other companies have similar practices. This committee is usually also responsible for transferring personnel between the various companies and for overseeing the overall salary and bonus system. In most Korean corporations, centralized planning, coordination, and decisionmaking are hallmarks of great importance.

Entrepreneurial Orientation

The fourth characteristic of the typical Korean corporation is a distinct entrepreneurial bent. A major reason for this can be found in the personalities of the founders and the nature of Korean society. The drive and ambition of founders like Chung of Hyundai and Lee of Samsung, the blend of traditional and contemporary values, and the unique nature of business-government relations in Korea (see Chapter 2) have created prime conditions for entrepreneurial efforts.

During the past thirty years many Korean businessmen have attempted to begin new companies. However, what separated the successful from the unsuccessful was often the entrepreneurial talents of the founder. As Kumho's President Park noted in our interview, "We [Korean entrepreneurs] would try new things and fail and sell the business and try again. . . . Hunger. Drive. Only entrepreneurs take the necessary risks to succeed."

Entrepreneurs in Korea succeeded for several reasons. To begin with, most successful founders began their companies with a clear vision of what they wanted their businesses to be. They chose their product lines carefully and then implemented highly developed business plans designed to meet these objectives.

Second, the successful founders exhibited good political skills. They convinced the Korean government that their plans had merit and would help the economic development of the country. Without this key support at the highest levels of the Korean government, the chaebols never would have received the necessary financing for their new ventures. (The vast majority of new financing came from the government or government-controlled banks, not from the stocks or venture capitalists.)

Third, successful founders and their managers pursued business aggressively and relentlessly. Chairman Kim of Daewoo, for example, is often described by associates as the hardest-working executive in Korea; he is said to never stop working on behalf of the company or looking for a new and profitable product or venture.

Fourth, the founders of successful ventures have a flair for making decisions and hiring and promoting the right people. One executive has observed that successful Korean CEOs relied heavily on their instincts in decisionmaking: "We Koreans are as sophisticated as the Americans and other international competitors, but we tend to follow our inner instincts much more." This is not to say that Korean executives tend to make hasty decisions; rather, their instinctual behavior is borne of years of watching and observing business markets around the world.

Finally, at least some of the success of these entrepreneurs can be traced to good fortune. Economic opportunities that are quickly exploited often lead to new opportunities. For example, recently Koreans spoke of the "age of the three lows"—meaning low oil prices, low currency valuation, and low interest rates. Because of favorable internal economic conditions and the concomitant rise in the value of the Japanese yen, Korean companies have been able to move quickly into Western markets and capture considerable market share.

An example of this entrepreneurial drive can be seen in the case of Lee Byung-Chull of Samsung, described in Chapter 2. Another example is Chairman Chung of Hyundai. In the early 1970s, Hyundai set out to build Korea's biggest shipyard. The company had no experience building ships, and experts were certain the venture would fail. Chairman Chung had made up his mind, however: "A ship has an engine inside and an exterior made of steel. . . . Ships resemble power plants, which Hyundai has built many times," he observed (Matsumoto 1986: 23). With these words he inspired his subordinates and went on to successfully accomplish the task. Chung succeeded for many reasons. He had market knowledge and a business plan, he had capable employees willing to work long hours to make the venture succeed, and he had government support that provided financing and a quasi-monopolistic business environment. In addition, he had an entrepreneurial drive and the instinct to recognize opportunity and plan accordingly. His story is repeated over and over in the history of modern Korean business enterprise.

Close Business-Government Relations

Like Japan, the economic foundations of modern Korea rest on a close and mutually beneficial relationship between business and government. Although the strength of this relationship is clearly diminishing, the fact remains that a key to the chaebols' success in the recent past was their usefulness to the government as an instrument for economic development. The government used its power through preferential loans and interest rates, through licensing authorizations, and through inclusion of certain companies in its recurring five-year economic development plans to select and then guide those chosen for success. Because of this link, successful chaebols needed to be "connected" in the right places. To be connected, companies had to support the incumbent political party, make donations to the right causes, and succeed with their sponsored ventures. Failure to accomplish any of these activities could—and sometimes did—lead to a termination of financing and immediate bankruptcy.

A case in point is the Kukje Group. Kukje was Korea's seventh-largest chaebol when it was forced into bankruptcy by the government in 1985. At the time of its liquidation (the group was split up and the assets assigned to other groups), Kukje had a diversified portfolio of profitable companies. It had 38,000 employees and an annual turnover of $1.5 billion. However, like most groups, it was highly leveraged and had borrowed considerably from the government.

In 1984 Kukje made a serious mistake: It offended the government of President Chun. During the Chun regime, it was a common practice for companies to pay quasi-taxes to such government-supported efforts as the *Saemaul Undong* (or New Village Movement), an organization originally created to aid in rural development but that by 1984 was run by President Chun's younger brother, and the Ilhae Foundation, a research organization focusing on issues of Korean reunification. It was widely charged that these payments represented bribes to the government in exchange for government support of the companies (Clifford 1988a). In any case, the president of Kukje, Yang Chang Mo, was seen by the government as not providing sufficient support to government-sanctioned causes. Specifically, his company "donated" only $400,000 to *Saemaul Undong* when other large chaebols were giving well over $1 million annually. Moreover, Yang refused to participate in a $40 million campaign drive for the Ilhae Foundation, which was named for Chun Doo Hwan's pseudonym and was closely associated with the president.

In any event, in December 1984 Korea First Bank (whose top officials were appointed by the Chun government) refused to honor Kukje's checks, sending a shockwave through the financial community. Short-term finance companies began calling in their debts, and Kukje was forced to scramble for funding. The company appealed to the government for help, but it was not forthcoming. The company was forced into bankruptcy. For the other chaebols, the message was clear: Both above and below the table, the government was not to be disobeyed. Currently, Yang is suing the government, charging corruption and attempting to reconstruct the company.

One way to remain connected has been for companies to hire top executives who were retiring from high government positions. Since government retirement age has historically been fifty-five and corporate retirement age among top executives is somewhat more flexible, this practice benefits both parties: The company gets a well-placed (and well-connected) bureaucrat, and the bureaucrat continues to earn income. Exhibit 3-2 shows the source of outside hires into the executive ranks for the major firms. Three things should be noted about this table. First, the largest number of outside hires are indeed from government, supporting the notion that government hires are useful for the companies. Second, however, companies also hire from the military (although this could be considered government hiring in view of the close military-government ties under Presidents Park and Chun) and from financial institutions. Finally, it is important to remember that many other countries, including the United States, engage in similar practices of hiring key government employees, although possibly not to the same extent as Korea.

A close relationship between business and government remains a hallmark of many of the major chaebols, and observers have called this relationship "Korea, Inc.," much like "Japan, Inc." A clear distinction between the two needs to be made, however. In Japan, the

Exhibit 3-2. Previous Occupations of Outside Hires for Top Managers.*

	Politicians	Bureaucrats	Military	Financiers
Samsung	—	1	2	1
Hyundai	—	2	3	2
Lucky-Goldstar	2	4	2	2
Daewoo	—	5	6	12
Sunkyong	—	1	—	1
Ssangyong	—	4	2	1

*All of the above managers were hired with a title of executive vice president or higher.
Source: Based on Joon Bae, "Ex-Bureaucrats and Ex-Military Men in the Financial World," Sin-Dong-A, August 1986, 403.

relationship between business and government is typically one of mutual consensus among relative equals on policy decisions. In Korea, government sets the policies, and businesses typically follow. It is certainly not an equal partnership. Government disfavor for whatever reason can bring about a loss of credit and financial ruin. In Japan, most conglomerates include banks as part of their organization structure and are thus assured of reliable sources of credit. As a result, it is sometimes said that Korea represents an unusual blend of free enterprise and state direction.

School Ties in Hiring

The final characteristic of many of Korea's major companies is the importance of educational credentials in career success. In South Korea, attending a prestigious college and to a lesser extent a prestigious high school is crucial for career advancement. Perhaps the three most prestigious universities are Seoul National University, Yonsei University, and Korea University, and graduation from one of these schools almost guarantees the student a job with one of the best companies.

The link between going to the right school and success is evident at Daewoo, where seven of the top nine executives (including the chairman) attended prestigious Kyunggi High School. Similarly, at Sunkyong, Seoul National University graduates currently occupy 50 percent of the group's directors and high-level officials (*Business Korea*, 1988a, 30). Exhibit 3–3 indicates the schools attended by the inner circle of top executives of seven chaebols, excluding founders and their successors. As can be seen, 62 percent of the highest executives in the seven companies attended Seoul National University. If Yonsei and Korea Universities are added, the percentage increases to 84 percent. This trend also can be seen in the middle and lower echelons of management, although at lower percentages.

When Korean managers are introduced, one of their first questions they ask each other concerns where they went to school. Discovering that both attended the same high school or university (even at different times) often brings an instant feeling of closeness. These ties help define who the employee is in the organization and provide a degree of status in a status-oriented society. They continue to affect the employee throughout his career.

Exhibit 3-3. Universities Attented by Top Executives of Major Chaebols.

	Universities				
Chaebol	Seoul National University	Yonsei University	Korea University	Military Academy	Others
Hyundai	1	3	3	—	—
Samsung	5	1	—	1	2
Lucky-Goldstar	11	1	—	—	3
Daewoo	7	1	1	—	—
Ssangyong	7	1	3	2	1
Sunkyong	6	1	—	—	1

Source: Based on Joon Bae, "The New Division Commanders of the Seven Chaebol Groups," *Sin-Dong-A* (April 1985: 524-48. In Hwan Ro, ed., *Directory of Businessmen in Korea* (Seoul: Federation of Korean Industries, 1985).

The major chaebol groups, then, tend to consist of six rather consistent characteristics that relate to personality and family relations, government relations, management style, and even past affiliations. As we shall see, these characteristics often come together to contribute to the growth and development of modern enterprise in Korea.

KOREAN CHAEBOL VERSUS JAPANESE KEIRETSU

Westerners often assume that few if any differences exist between Korean companies and their Japanese counterparts (generally referred since the war as *keiretsu*, or loosely-coupled yet interrelated groups of companies, such as the Sumitomo Group or the Mitsui Group). Indeed, both exist in East Asian countries and are influenced by similar cultural roots. Moreover, many of today's Korean companies and Korean governmental agencies were established during Japanese occupation. Although a number of similarities can be noted, several distinct differences exist.

First and foremost among these differences is the *nature of ownership* of the chaebols and keiretsus. In Korea most companies are closely held by family members. Many large business groups in Japan are also family enterprises (especially those founded before World War II, when such conglomerates were referred to as *zaibatsu*), but the percentage of family shares in contemporary Japanese conglomerates is now typically much smaller. Moreover, the definition of *family* is different in Japan and Korea. In Korea family members are determined by blood relationships (consanguinity), whereas Japan has two different definitions of family—one based on blood relationships and another based on household or clan relationships. In most cases, clan relationship, not blood, determines inheritance and succession. In Korea family members typically own a large share of the company and the determination of who is part of the family is narrow; therefore, a greater concentration of wealth or assets is found in fewer hands.

As a result of this, a second difference between the two countries emerges—namely, the increased *centralization of power* in the hands of the CEOs in Korea compared to Japan. Korean CEOs are seldom challenged, however politely; their decisions are absolute. This characteristic has allowed many Korean firms to move more quickly or decisively than their Japanese counterparts on many occasions because less time is spent on consensus-building among people at various levels of the organization. This centralization also opens greater possibilities for strategic errors due to hasty decisions or decisions made without sufficient information. Based on our observations, executives from both countries collect an enormous amount of information about business events; the Japanese, however, seem to make somewhat greater use of this information than their Korean counterparts.

As a result of extensive family ownership of Korean enterprises, the majority of top managers in Korea are family members. Hence, the percentage of *professional managers* who work their way to the top is considerably higher in Japan than in Korea. Much of this difference can be attributed to the relative newness of the Korean companies (many of the founders are still alive, whereas many of the major Japanese companies are several hundred years old), and as time goes on a greater percentage of professional managers can be expected.

A fourth difference is the nature of *business-government relationships*. As was seen earlier, this relationship has a decidedly superior-subordinate nature in Korea compared to Japan, although this too is changing slowly under the new government. In Japan this relationship (especially with the Ministry of International Trade and Industry) is not completely equal but is at least a little less one-sided than it has been in Korea. Because of the relationship with the government, a fifth difference was noted above—namely, the *nature of financing*. Most borrowing for new ventures in Korea has been from the government, while in Japan far more borrowing is from group-connected banks, which gives Japanese concerns greater freedom than their Korean counterparts.

Finally, many similarities exist in the two countries' approaches to *human resource management*, but several differences can also be noted. These differences involve corporate approaches to lifetime employment guarantees, bonus payments, and retirement policies and are discussed in detail in Chapter 7. Thus, although a number of similarities can be found across the two cultures, clear differences must be recognized because they influence both the day-to-day operations and the long-term strategic planning carried out by major corporations in Korea and Japan. Many of these differences are examined as we continue exploring how Korean corporations approach strategy, management, and personnel policies.

4 CORPORATE PROFILES
The Big Four

To understand how the major companies of Korea arrived on the international scene it is helpful to examine several chaebols to see how they developed strategies for growth and development. It is also important to look at the size, diversity, and market power of the major players in the field. This chapter reviews the histories of the so-called Big Four—Samsung, Hyundai, Lucky-Goldstar, and Daewoo. Space does not permit a review of all of the chaebols, but these four are representative of other major Korean companies. Chapter 5 will then provide a more detailed examination of the chaebols' approach to corporate strategy and global competition. We begin with Samsung, Korea's largest company.

SAMSUNG: A DRIVE FOR PERFECTION

As was shown in Chapter 2, from its inauspicious beginning in 1938 and its rebirth in 1951, the Samsung Group grew as Korea grew under the leadership of Lee Byung-Chull. Following the Korean War, the company in the 1950s provided basic necessities to resupply a war-torn country. Cheil Sugar & Co., Ltd. was founded in 1953, followed closely by Cheil Wool Textile Co., Ltd. in 1954. Interestingly, several of Lee's initial ventures were named *Cheil* (meaning "number one" in Korean) to reflect the founder's desire to be the best. Lee once observed, "Money is not what I pursued. Instead, I have only striven to be the best in whatever business I chose" (*Business Korea* 1987: 47).

Emphasis on Technological Development

As Korea's standard of living rose, Samsung moved into the service sector with businesses in insurance, broadcasting, securities, and even a department store. By the end of the 1960s Samsung had an annual turnover of $100 million. In the 1970s the company entered electronics (initially black and white televisions) and heavy industries (shipbuilding and petrochemicals), and by the end of the decade Samsung's combined turnover reached $3 billion. In the 1980s more emphasis was placed on high-technology ventures. Samsung Semiconductor and Telecommunications Co., established in 1978, became the first Korean company to manufacture the 64K DRAM chip, followed shortly by the 256K and 1 MB chips. In 1986 Samsung Aerospace was designated by the government as systems integrator for the F-16 fighter-plane project.

To capitalize on its competitive edge in high technology both in semiconductors and genetic engineering, Samsung has established twelve research centers in Korea and two in the United States. In 1987 it established the Samsung Advanced Institute of Technology with research laboratories in electronics, computers and communications, materials and devices, semiconductors and telecommunications, chemistry and aerospace engineering. The Institute currently has a staff of about 2,700.

A Global Outlook

Samsung also has an ambitious plan to become a truly international corporation. In 1982 it opened a television assembly facility in Portugal with a capacity of 300,000 units for sale within the European common market. This was followed in 1984 with a $25 million plant in New Jersey that produces 1 million televisions and about 400,000 microwave overns per year. In 1987 another $25 million facility was opened in England with a capacity for 300,000 VCRs, 400,000 color televisions, and 300,000 microwave ovens. Further expansion is proceeding or anticipated in Thailand and other less-developed countries (such as China), and the company's goal is to double its exports (from $2.2 billion to $5 billion) by the early 1990s, becoming one of the top seven electronics manufacturers in the world (*Business Korea* 1988e).

Today the Samsung Group comprises twenty-six affiliated companies with a little over 160,000 employees. Since Lee's death in 1987 the group has been managed by his third son, Lee Kun-Hee; 1987 sales were $24 billion (*Forbes* 1988). The group's businesses can be divided into seven divergent fields: trade, electronics, heavy industries and chemicals, precision instruments, food processing and textiles, service, and culture and welfare. The principal companies, their products, and employees are shown in Exhibit 4–1. Clearly, the Samsung Group is a highly diversified and adaptive enterprise that competes effectively in the global economy.

HYUNDAI: THE CAN-DO SPIRIT

The story of Hyundai is the story of Chung Ju-Yung. Until a few years ago, Hyundai was little known in the West. Then came the Hyundai Excel, the fastest-selling import in both the United States and Canada when introduced. Western consumers now are beginning to see the new Hyundai microcomputers. But although name recognition for this and other Korean companies may be a recent phenomenon, the strength and diversity—and success—of the Hyundai Group have a long tradition.

Chung Ju-yung: From Bricklayer to Chairman

Although Lee Byung-Chull was born to a moderately wealthy family, Chung Ju-yung was born to a poor, rural farming family in 1915. With little formal education, he learned various manual labor skills and in the 1940s established a truck and motor service business. In 1947 he formed Hyundai Engineering and Construction Company, focusing on the construction of dams, roads, harbors, and housing projects. As the first Korean construction company to win overseas contracts, Hyundai undertook highway projects in Thailand, harbor dredging in South Vietnam and Australia, bridges in Alaska, and

Exhibit 4-1. Principal Business Fields, Companies, and Employees of the Samsung Group.

Business Field and Company	Main Products or Services	Number of Employees
Trade		
Samsung Co., Ltd.	Exports, imports, natural resource development	4,360
Electronics		
Samsung Electronics Co., Ltd.	Color and black-and-white television, VCRs, stereo systems, home appliances, industrial electronic equipment	19,955
Samsung Electron Devices Co., Ltd.	Picture tubes, CRTs for data display, display monitors, receiving tubes, transistors, diodes, computers	6,567
Samsung Electro-Mechanics Co., Ltd.	VHF and UHF tuners, condensers, ceramic capacitors, speakers, deck mechanisms	6,093
Samsung Corning Co., Ltd.	Television glass bulbs, electronic gun-mounts, glass rods, glass bulbs for computer display	2,397
Samsung Semiconductor & Telecommunications Co., Ltd.	64K DRAM, 256K DRAM, and 1 MB DRAM semiconductors, optical cable and fibers, electronic switching systems, computers, facsimiles	10,639
Heavy Industry and Chemicals		
Samsung Shipbuilding & Heavy Industries Co., Ltd.	Industrial machinery and equipment, structure steel, shipbuilding and offshore structures	6,983
Samsung Petrochemical Co., Ltd.	Purified Terephthalic Acid	381
Samsung Construction Co., Ltd.	Civil engineering, architectural construction, and plant installation	11,507

Company	Products/Services	
Korea Engineering Co., Ltd.	Plant engineering	590
Chonju Paper Manufacturing Co., Ltd.	Newsprint, printing paper, bleached ground wood pulp	1,201
Precision Instruments		
Samsung Aerospace Industries, Ltd.	Jet-engines, electro-optics equipment, cameras, industrial robots, process control systems, computer peripherals	2,289
Samsung Watch Co., Ltd.	Digital and analog watches, electronic display boards	830
Food Processing and Textiles		
Cheil Sugar & Co., Ltd.	Sugar, MSG, flour, IMP, GMP, cut pork, formulated feed, soybean meal, begetable oil, processed meat, premix organic fertilizers	4,131
Cheil Wool Textile Co., Ltd.	Worsted textiles, woolen textiles, men and women's garments, knitwear, blankets	3,645
Cheil Synthetic Textiles Co., Ltd.	Polyester staple fiber, polyester filament	2,713
Services		
Dongbang Life Insurance Co., Ltd.	Individual and group life insurance	52,529
Aukuk Fire & Marine Insurance Co. Ltd.	Fire, marine, and casuality insurance	1,234
Hotel Shilla Co., Ltd.	Hotel services	1,291
Shinsegae Department Store Co., Ltd.	Consumer retail	1,578
Culture and Social Welfare		
Joong-ang Development Co., Ltd.	Development of groundwater resources	1,550
Joong-ang Daily News Co., Ltd.	Daily newspaper, magazines	1,019

Source: Adapted from *Samsung: Its Role and Activities as a General Trading Company: 1986–1987* (Seoul, 1987): 46–47.

housing complexes in Guam. The company became increasingly adept at larger and more complex projects and could successfully compete internationally because it used cheap, hard-working labor and had a tradition of timely completion dates.

In 1968 Chairman Chung decided to enter the automobile industry and established Hyundai Motor Company to assemble Ford passenger cars for sale locally. With this experience, Hyundai designed and produced (with technical assistance from Mitsubishi) Korea's first integrated passenger car, the Pony. In 1983 the midsized Steller model was introduced, and by 1988 Hyundai was producing a luxury sedan, the Grandeur, under license from Mitsubishi. A redesigned version of the Pony Excel was introduced first into Canada in 1986 and into the United States a year later. The Steller has also been sold in Canada. More recently, a newly designed Hyundai Sonata has been introduced to the North American market. The Sonata is designed as a more up-scale medium-sized car to compete with many of the Japanese imports, such as the Honda Accord and the Toyota Camry (*Business Korea* 1988d).

Growth through Diversification

In 1973 Hyundai Heavy Industries Co., Ltd. was formed as a major shipbuilding enterprise, one of the largest in the world, and soon won shipbuilding contracts away from Japanese and Western European companies with its highly skilled labor force and competitive prices. Meanwhile, the company's construction business expanded significantly in the Middle East. This effort was highlighted by the completion of the $1.1 billion Jubail Industrial Harbor Project in Saudi Arabia.

As these companies grew and uncovered new economic opportunities, many units were spun off as independent companies; these included Hyundai Engine & Machinery Co., Hyundai Electrical Engineering Co., Ltd., and Hyundai Rolling Stock Co., Ltd. The group also acquired Inchon Iron & Steel Co., Ltd. and Aluminum of Korea, Ltd. In 1976 the Hyundai Corporation was formed as the group's general trading company, and in the late 1970s Hyundai Electronics Industries Co., Ltd. was formed as Chairman Chung decided to take the company into high technology. In 1984 Hyundai Offshore and Engineering Co., Ltd. was formed to pursue the increasing business in offshore drilling platforms. A recent listing of Hyundai's business interests is shown in Exhibit 4–2.

Exhibit 4-2. Principal Business Fields and Companies of the Hyundai Group.

Business Field and Company	Main Products or Services
Shipbuilding and Heavy Industries	
Hyundai Heavy Industries Co., Ltd.	Shipbuilding and sales of tankers, containerships, drilling rigs; industrial plants and steel fabrication
Hyundai Mipo Dockyard Co., Ltd.	Ship repair and ship conversion
Engineering and Construction	
Hyundai Engineering & Construction Co., Ltd.	General contracting, design, and construction
Halla Construction Co., Ltd.	Construction and design of industrial plants, marine and offshore facilities, civil works, building and housing, landscaping
Hyundai Engineering Co., Ltd.	Feasibility studies, engineering and design, project management, procurement, financial arrangement, computer analysis, construction, supervision, inspection and quality assurance in various engineering fields
Korea Urban Development Co., Ltd.	Construction related to civil and architectural engineering works including residential houses, buildings, city planning, water supply and plumbing systems, landscaping; real estate management
Hankook Pavement Construction Co., Ltd.	Ascon products, construction materials, construction realted to civil and architectural engineering works
Hyundai Offshore & Engineering Co., Ltd.	Onshore steel structures for high-rise buildings, bridges and industrial plants; offshore steel structures for the offshore oil development

(Exhibit 4-2. continued overleaf)

Exhibit 4-2. *continued*

Business Field and Company	Main Products or Services
International Trading	
Hyundai Corporation	Marketing and trading of all products and services of Hyundai Group and other Korean firms; procurement and import of natural resources through overseas investment and joint venture activities; providing technical and financial assistance to overseas enterprises
Vehicles and Rolling Stock	
Hyundai Motor Company	Passenger cars and commercial vehicles
Hyundai Rolling Stock Co., Ltd.	Locomotives and railway carriages
Hyundai Motor Service Co., Ltd.	Automotive parts and repair services
Electronic and Electrical Equipment	
Hyundai Electrical Engineering Co., Ltd.	Transformers, generators, motors and circuit breakers for industrial and marine use
Hyundai Electronics Industries Co., Ltd.	Semiconductor, electronics systems, information systems, office automation, home electronics
Machinery; Steel and Metal Products	
Hyundai Engine & Machinery Co., Ltd.	Engines for ships and industrial use; various industrial machinery
Inchon Iron & Steel Co., Ltd.	Steel and iron products; purchasing and scrapping of second-hand vessels
Hyundai Precision & Industry Co., Ltd.	Automotive parts; containers; valves and castings
Hyundai Pipe Co., Ltd.	Steel pipes
Korea Flange Co., Ltd.	Flanges, gratings, fittings

Aluminium of Korea, Ltd.   Refining of aluminium

Seohan Development Co., Ltd.   Welding materials and calcium carbides

Construction Materials and Furniture

Hyundai Cement Co., Ltd.   Cement; mining development

Hyundai Wood Industries Co., Ltd.   Building materials, lumber goods, and furniture

Dongsu Industrial Co., Ltd.   Cement products; ceramic tiles

Keumkang, Ltd.   Asbestos cement, noncombustible building materials; construction related to civil and architectural engineering works

Korea Chemical Co., Ltd.   Paints; resins for organic coating

Keumkang Development Industrial Co., Ltd.   Production of foods and garments; ticketing services; tourist hotel proprietorship

Shipping and Services

Hyundai Merchant Marine Co., Ltd.   Liner and tramper cargo services, vessel chartering, ship brokering, agency services, trading and related services; culture and welfare

Source: Adapted from *Hyundai Heavy Industries Co., Ltd. Report* (Seoul, 1985): 69–70.

To increase the number of engineering students in Korea, Chung established the Ulsan Institute of Technology in 1977, and in the same year donated one-half of his holdings in the parent company, Hyundai Engineering and Construction Company (worth $70 million), to his newly created Asan Foundation to help fund rural hospitals, educational scholarships, and social welfare programs. Chung now serves as a member of the board of directors of Korea University, where he once worked as a bricklayer as a young man in the 1930s.

Today Hyundai is a thriving enterprise, but its close family ownership and limited financial reporting make its actual value difficult to estimate. In determining the International *Fortune* 500, *Fortune* magazine could only report separate data for Hyundai Motor and Hyundai Heavy Industries and, as such, did not rank the group highly (*Fortune* 1988). These two companies within the Hyundai Group are indeed sizable: Hyundai Motor by itself ranks as the 191st largest company in sales outside the United States, with sales of $3.4 billion, net income of $72.3 million, and 29,000 employees in 1987; and Hyundai Heavy Industries by itself ranked 225th in the world, with sales of $2.9 billion, net income of $19.3 million, and 48,200 employees. Meanwhile, *Forbes* (1988) estimated total group sales for 1987 at $22.7 billion, while total employment can be estimated from company documents at over 140,000.

LUCKY-GOLDSTAR: HARMONY AND INNOVATION

Whereas Samsung's origins can be traced to general trading and Hyundai's to construction, Lucky-Goldstar's early beginnings were in the field of chemistry. Founded by Koo In-Whoi in 1947, the Lucky Chemical Company (later Lucky, Ltd.) initially manufactured cosmetics (especially facial creams). The company later expanded into plastics (including combs, toothbrushes, and plastic basins). After the Korean War, the predominantly home products company added toothpaste and laundry detergent. A trading company was established in 1953, followed by the creation of Goldstar Co., Ltd. in 1958 to produce radios, refrigerators (1965), and televisions (1966). An oil refinery was established in 1967. From here, the company continued to grow as a "dual-track" entity, stressing product innovations in both chemistry (through Lucky, Ltd.) and electronics (through Goldstar Co., Ltd.) and later adding services and public welfare to its areas of responsibility.

Today, the group consists of twenty-nine affiliated companies and is managed by the dynamic Chairman Koo Cha-Kyung (see Exhibit 4–3). Sales for 1987 totalled $16 billion, while employment stands at an estimated 88,400 (*Fortune* 1988; *Forbes* 1988). The group is ranked thirty-second in the world in terms of total sales in the 1988 Fortune International 500.

A Concern for People

Lucky-Goldstar as a group differs in several important respects from most other Korean enterprises. First, while employees of the company are clearly proud of the achievements of the founder (Koo In-Whoi), there is little of the personality cult that typifies many other chaebols. Moreover, the group is somewhat more decentralized than most other groups. Significant efforts have been made to develop competent professional managers capable of managing various businesses. Major strategic decisions are still made in the office of the chairman, but within these guidelines individual companies are free to pursue their businesses as they see fit. Finally, Lucky-Goldstar is often described as a conservative, stable company that avoids risky ventures and stresses group harmony in all endeavors (the company motto is *inhwa*, or group harmony). In this sense, it has less of the "department store mentality" that characterizes groups that spread themselves thinly into many new and often unrelated areas. Most of Lucky-Goldstar's new ventures are logical extensions of existing businesses. For example, in our interviews with Kwon Moon-Koo, senior managing director of the chairman's office, he noted that the chairman stresses autonomy in business decisions for each company of the group and careful value-added analyses before new ventures are initiated. There is considerable emphasis on the sustainability of the group and its companies in all decisions. Finally, Mr. Kwon emphasized the importance of competitiveness in all decisions affecting the marketplace; Lucky-Goldstar intends to grow and prosper.

Exhibit 4–3. Principal Business Groups and Companies of the Lucky-Goldstar Group.

Chemistry and Resources

Lucky, Ltd.
Honam Oil Refinery Co., Ltd.
Lucky Advanced Materials, Inc.
Korea Mining & Smelting Co., Ltd.

Electric and Electronics

Goldstar Co., Ltd.
Goldstar Semiconductor, Ltd.
Goldstar Electronics Co., Ltd.
Goldstar Telecommunication Co., Ltd.
Goldstar Electric Co., Ltd.
Goldstar Alps Electronics Co., Ltd.
Goldstar Precision Co., Ltd.
Goldstar Industrial Systems Co., Ltd.
Goldstar Instrument & Electric Co., Ltd.
Goldstar Electric Machinery Co., Ltd.
Goldstar Honeywell Co., Ltd.
Goldstar Cable Co., Ltd.

Services

Lucky-Goldstar International Corp.
Lucky Securities Co., Ltd.
Pan Korea Insurance Co., Ltd.
Goldstar Investment & Finance Corp.
Pusan Investment & Finance Corp.
Lucky Development Co., Ltd.
Lucky Engineering Co., Ltd.
Hee Sung Co., Ltd.
LG Ad, Inc.

Public Services & Sports

Lucky-Goldstar Sports
Yonam Foundation
Yonam Junior College of Engineering
Yonam Junior College of Livestock and Horticulture

Source: Adapted from *1988 Goldstar Company Report* (Seoul), 63.

In 1986–87 the major divisions of the Goldstar (electronics) part of Lucky-Goldstar were reorganized into five groups (see Exhibit 4–4). This reorganization was designed to reposition the company to better take advantage of the dynamic changes both in technology and the marketplace in electronics. As a result, Goldstar emerged with five relatively autonomous sectors in consumer products, computer and communications, electronic devices, industrial systems, and semiconductors. In this reorganization, corporate executives paid close attention to the strategic direction of Samsung. In fact, it is indeed ironic that when Goldstar executives are asked who their primary competitor is, the answer they give is not Mitsubishi or Hewlett-Packard but Samsung. Similarly, Samsung sees Goldstar and not Japan or the United States, as its primary competitor.

Commitment to Research and Development

Like Samsung, the Lucky-Goldstar Group is committed to applied research. To understand how successful such a company can be when the effort is made, consider the history of accomplishments of only the Goldstar side of the group, shown in Exhibit 4–5. To maintain such a record, Lucky-Goldstar invests heavily in research, spending $348 million in 1986 and $470 in 1987. This represents 5 percent of total sales (compared to 3 percent for similar companies), and plans are in place to increase this to 7 percent by 1998.

The company maintains numerous research labs, but its major efforts are centered in its Central Research Institute in Taedok (established in 1979), which carries out research in chemical technologies and advanced material sciences, and in a major R&D complex in Anyang (established in 1985), which focuses on electronics research. The authors' own visit to the Anyang facility was impressive in terms of the vitality and ambition of the researchers. The entire group has 2,500 researchers (over 100 with Ph.D.s) and plans to have a total of 10,000 researchers by 1998. As Koo Cha-Hak (Lucky-Goldstar Group 1988: 5), vice chairman of the Lucky-Goldstar Group and CEO of Goldstar, notes, "Our goal is to become nothing less than the #1 electronics manufacturer in the world, and we are striving to achieve this goal through strict attention to quality, a commitment to efficiency and through strategic management."

Exhibit 4-4. 1987 Reorganization of Goldstar Consumer and Industrial Electronics.

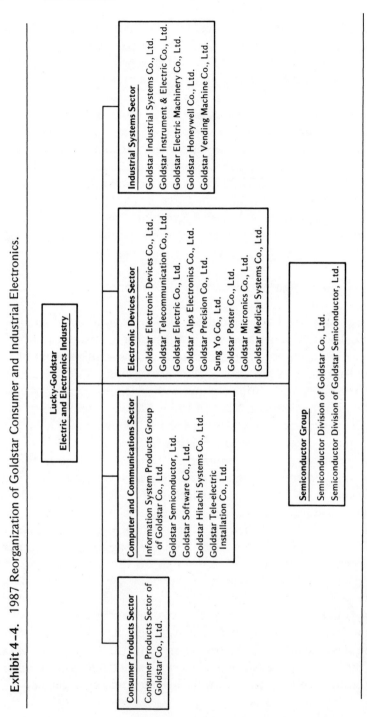

**Lucky-Goldstar
Electric and Electronics Industry**

Consumer Products Sector

Consumer Products Sector of Goldstar Co., Ltd.

Computer and Communications Sector

Information System Products Group of Goldstar Co., Ltd.
Goldstar Semiconductor, Ltd.
Goldstar Software Co., Ltd.
Goldstar Hitachi Systems Co., Ltd.
Goldstar Tele-electric Installation Co., Ltd.

Electronic Devices Sector

Goldstar Electronic Devices Co., Ltd.
Goldstar Telecommunication Co., Ltd.
Goldstar Electric Co., Ltd.
Goldstar Alps Electronics Co., Ltd.
Goldstar Precision Co., Ltd.
Sung Yo Co., Ltd.
Goldstar Poster Co., Ltd.
Goldstar Micronics Co., Ltd.
Goldstar Medical Systems Co., Ltd.

Industrial Systems Sector

Goldstar Industrial Systems Co., Ltd.
Goldstar Instrument & Electric Co., Ltd.
Goldstar Electric Machinery Co., Ltd.
Goldstar Honeywell Co., Ltd.
Goldstar Vending Machine Co., Ltd.

Semiconductor Group

Semiconductor Division of Goldstar Co., Ltd.
Semiconductor Division of Goldstar Semiconductor, Ltd.

Source: Adapted from *1988 Goldstar Company Report* (Seoul), pp. 6–7.

Exhibit 4-5. Notable Accomplishments of Goldstar.

1958	Founded.
1959	Produced Korea's first radio.
1965	Manufactured Korea's first refrigerator.
1966	Manufactured Korea's first television.
1968	First overseas branch established in New York.
	Produced Korea's first elevator and escalator.
1969	Manufactured Korea's first washing machine and air conditioner.
1975	Established Korea's first private R&D facility, the Goldstar Central Research Laboratory.
1976	Founded Goldstar Semiconductor.
1978	Became Korea's first electronics company with exports exceeding $100 million.
1979	Developed the nation's first computerized color television.
1980	Developed Korea's first electronic memory typewriter.
1981	Developed Korea's first electronic VCR.
1982	Completed Goldstar America's color television production facility in Huntsville, Alabama.
	Manufactured the nation's first microcomputer.
	Produced the first Korean cable television broadcasting system.
1983	Founded the Goldstar Design Center, the first such center in the Korean electronics industry.
	Manufactured Korea's first compact disk player.
	Developed Korea's first direct broadcasting system.
	Goldstar Instrument and Electric developed Korea's first programmable controller.
1984	Produced Korea's first protable VCR.
	Produced Korea's first digital color television.
1985	Produced Korea's first 8mm camcorder.
	Developed a 3.5 inch hard disk drive (HDD) for the fourth time in the world and 8 mm VTR tapes for the second time in the world.
	Manufactured Korea's first laser printer.
1986	Goldstar Europe established in Worms, West Germany.

Source: Adapted from *1988 Goldstar Company Report* (Seoul), 62.

Goldstar also has been aggressive in overseas production. In 1982 it opened what has become a major manufacturing plant in Huntsville, Alabama, which now manufactures 1 million color televisions and 500,000 microwave ovens for sale in North and South America.

This was the first major manufacturing facility built in the United States by a Korean company. Rejection rates at the plant are described as one of the lowest in the world and employee absenteeism is about 1 percent, compared to the U.S. national average of 5 percent (Lucky-Goldstar Group 1987c, 19). A second facility was opened in Worms, West Germany, in 1987 with annual capacities of 300,000 televisions and 400,000 VCRs. Due to the success of these two ventures, further international facilities are planned. In 1989 Goldstar announced plans to build a television manufacturing facility in China, the first such venture for a Korean company.

DAEWOO: FROM TEXTILES
TO CARS AND COMPUTERS

Founded in 1967 as a small textile trading company with an investment of $18,000 and four employees, Daewoo has grown in two short decades into a 120,000-employee organization with fifty-five affiliated companies and sales of $16 billion. Paid-in capital exceeds $2.2 billion, and exports for 1988 were around $4 billion (*Fortune* 1988; W. C. Kim 1988). If we are looking for an example of entrepreneurism in a Korean firm, clearly Daewoo is a good place to start.

Daewoo began by exporting fabrics to Southeast Asia. First-year sales were $580,000; two years later (1969) sales had reached $4 million. The company soon was producing textiles and had developed a reputation for high-quality, low-priced merchandise. Sears, Roebuck of the United States became Daewoo's first major international customer, followed quickly by J. C. Penney and Montgomery Ward. By 1972 the company was awarded 30 percent of the total U.S. import quota for textile products. By 1975 Daewoo was one of Korea's most profitable companies.

Expansion through Acquisition
and Joint Ventures

From this firm manufacturing base, Daewoo (which means "great universe" in Korean) moved into its second phase of development by initiating a series of fourteen acquisitions. Throughout, the strategy was the same and throughout it was successful: take over an ailing company, improve the management system and product quality, and turn the company around. In fact, one of the hallmarks of Daewoo is superior production capability. As a foreign observer for *Asian Finance* concluded, "Anyone who looks, for example, at Daewoo Electronics' TV production facilities at Gumi, the assembly lines at Daewoo Motor, the plants of the Korea Steel Chemical Co., or the shipyard at Okpo will have little doubt that here is production capability at its best" (Roy 1985, 65).

The first major takeover occurred in 1975, when Korean President Park asked Daewoo to acquire a state-owned machinery plant that had been losing money for thirty-seven years. Kim Woo-Choong, founder of Daewoo, changed the name of the company to Daewoo Heavy Industries and took personal control of the new company. Within one year, the company broke even and by the second year it began paying dividends. Shortly thereafter, President Park asked Kim to take over Okpo Shipbuilding Company, renamed Daewoo Shipbuilding and Heavy Machinery, Ltd. Kim invested $500 million in completing the facility, which today ranks as one of the world's largest and finest shipbuilding entities. Finally, Daewoo took over Saehan Motor Company, renaming it Daewoo Motor Company, in 1979. Again, through Kim's efforts, the enterprise was transformed into one of Korea's two largest auto companies. Since 1986 Daewoo has built the successful Pontiac LeMans for the U.S. market (production capacity 167,000) and in 1987 began exporting the LeMans to Taiwan and Canada.

Based on the success of the Daewoo-General Motors partnership, Daewoo began in the 1980s a series of joint ventures. Today, approximately twenty of the fifty-five companies of the group are joint ventures. Daewoo teamed up with General Dynamics to manufacture fuselages and equipment for the F-16 and with Boeing to assemble fuselages and wing parts for the 737, 747, and 767. Forklifts and construction equipment are made with Caterpillar. Optical fiber, cable, and telephone switching systems are built in partnership with Northern Telecom, while Daewoo Electronics builds motors for General Electric and will soon establish the first Asian manufacturing facility (for 300,000 microwave ovens) in France in partnership with JCB Participation.

Through this three-pronged strategy of company creation, company acquisition, and joint ventures, Daewoo continues to grow (approximately 20 percent per year) and develop into one of the world's most dynamic companies. In 1987 it ranked thirty-fifth in the world in the *Fortune* International 500, up from thirty-ninth in 1986. A listing of the principal companies within the Daewoo Group is shown in Exhibit 4-6. This exhibit reflects the group's realignment in November 1987.

The interrelationships between the various companies in the group can also be informative. As can be seen in Exhibit 4-7, many of the companies have sizable investments from other Daewoo companies, but the interlocking nature of this relationship, combined with the high rate of corporate borrowing, increases the risks of serious financial problems. For example, when Daewoo Shipbuilding experienced financial difficulties in 1988-89 and sought government assistance, the consequences could be felt by Daewoo Heavy Industries, Daewoo Corporation, and the government's Korea Development Bank—all of whom had substantial investments in shipbuilding (Clifford 1988d).

Kim Woo-Choong: The Consummate Entrepreneur

In the case of Daewoo, as in the case of most of the chaebols, the success of the company can be traced directly to the drive, skill, and entrepreneurial spirit of its founder, Kim Woo-Choong. Chairman Kim was born in 1936 in Taegu and was raised during the period of both the Japanese occupation and the Korean War. He is known in Korea as perhaps the hardest-working executive in the country. He sleeps four hours a night, works 100 hours per week, and travels over 200 days per year. By his own admission, he has not taken a vacation in thirty years (Yates 1985; Roy 1985; Caulkin 1986). Indeed, he recently commented "I certainly expect Daewoo people to work hard. But most of them know that in the twenty-one years since I founded Daewoo, I have taken no time off—except for the morning of my daughter's recent wedding" (W. C. Kim 1988: 8). He is up every morning at 5:30—"breakfasting with my family is very important to me"—and prefers Sunday morning meetings so as not to interrupt productive working hours. He does not drink or play golf or tennis, and in the early 1980s he turned over all of his personal business assets (estimated at between $40 to $50 million) to an independent cultural and medical foundation. Because of such exploits and his business success, Chairman Kim has become an oft-cited role

Exhibit 4-6. 1987 Daewoo Reorganization.

Division	Company
Trading and construction	Daewoo Corporation Keangnam Enterprises, Ltd. Kyungnam Metal Co., Ltd. Daewoo Engineering Co.
Machinery	Daewoo Heavy Industries, Ltd. Daewoo-Sikorsky Aerospace, Ltd. Daewoo Precision Industries, Ltd.
Electric and electronics	Daewoo Electronics Co., Ltd. Daewoo Carrier Corporation Daewoo Electric Motor Industries, Ltd. Orion Electric Co., Ltd. Daewoo Electronic Components Co., Ltd.
Telecommunications	Daewoo Telecom Co., Ltd.
Automotive	Daewoo Motor Co., Ltd.
Automotive parts	Daewoo Automotive Components, Ltd. Daewoo HMS Industries, Ltd. Koram Plastics Co., Ltd. Dongheung Electric Co., Ltd.
Shipbuilding	Daewoo Shipbuilding & Heavy Machinery, Ltd. Shina Shipbuilding Co., Ltd. Daewoo-ITT Engineered Products, Ltd.
Chemicals	Korea Steel Chemical Co., Ltd. Pungkuk Oil Co., Ltd.
Finance	Daewoo Securities Co., Ltd. Daewoo Research Institute Daewoo Investment & Finance Corp.
Others	Dongwoo Development Co., Ltd. Sorak Development Co., Ltd.

Source: Adapted from *News from Daewoo* (Seoul, Winter 1987–88), 8.

Exhibit 4–7. Interlocking Patterns of Financial Control at Daewoo.

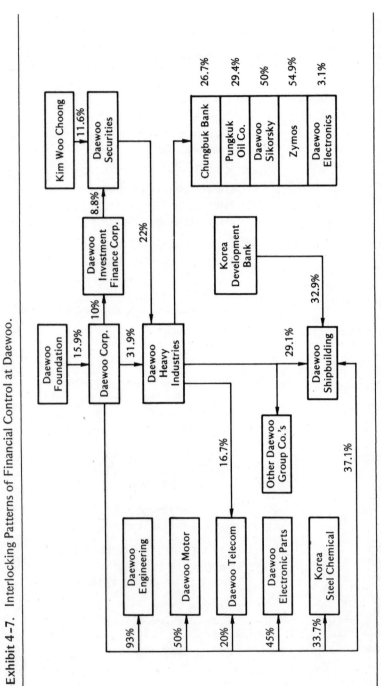

Source: Far Eastern Economic Review (December 8, 1988): 53. Reprinted by permission of the Review Publishing Company, Ltd., Hong Kong.

model and folk hero to many Korean managers both inside and outside Daewoo.

In describing his approach to management, Kim (1988) frequently refers to the "Daewoo spirit." This spirit (often seen hanging in calligraphy on the walls of various Daewoo executives) is comprised of three elements: creativity, challenge, and sacrifice. Daewoo employees tell the outsider that these words are more than an empty slogan; they indicate deeply felt beliefs that often guide employee behavior. During this period in Korean economic development, these three qualities are felt to be essential if the company and the country are to attain their aspirations. Kim also talks about Daewoo's emphasis on *coprosperity.* By this he means that every company has a responsibility to deliver equitable benefits to workers, customers, suppliers, partners, and the government. In this way, harmony is preserved, and every sector of the culture benefits.

Kim (1988, 4) attributes the success of Daewoo to three related attributes. First, he notes that the company is market-driven: "At the time of our founding as a textile trading company, I saw tremendous international possibilities. When I entered the American market, I decided to go directly to independent retailers and chain stores. I avoided Japanese middlemen, which was an uncommon practice for Koreans at that time. I also learned the benefits of market research and innovation. We developed new styles and fabrics, rather than passively meeting buyer demands. I believe that pioneering new markets is as important as creating new technology."

Second, Kim (1988, 4–5) describes Daewoo as a company that is "flexible, ready to adjust, and innovative. . . . We have not waited for things to happen. We have capitalized upon changing opportunities." Daewoo, like many other Korean companies, accommodates environmental changes in a way that often seems ahead of the trends. When some companies were getting out of oil, for example, Kim bought an oil refinery in Belgium. He then proceeded to increase his business in Third World countries where he could trade his products for crude oil. Since he had his own refinery, he was less susceptible to price changes on the world spot market, thereby increasing both his security and profitability (Kraar 1987).

Third, Kim is known as a risk-taker (like Chairman Chung at Hyundai). In Korean, *risk* translates into a word that combines the characters for *crisis* and *chance.* In other words, any crisis facing a company can also be thought of as an opportunity if handled correctly. When many Korean companies were engaged in construction work in the Middle East, for example, Kim felt he had greater opportunities (and less competition) contracting in Africa. As Kim (1988, 5) notes "Of course, the African market was smaller and less stable, both financially and politically. But the greater the risk, the greater the chance for accomplishments and profits." As a result, Daewoo ended up with $2 billion in construction contracts in Libya. Kim believes that if there is no risk, there is no money. Hence, the question becomes how one *manages* the risk. The way to manage the risk in Libya is to require payment in advance. Such an approach to business management has resulted in Daewoo's accounting for nearly 10 percent of Korea's exports over the past twenty years.

These descriptions concerning the founding and development of Samsung, Hyundai, Lucky-Goldstar, and Daewoo illustrate how Korean managers and employees, working in concert, can contribute to rapid industrial progress through hard work, initiative, and seizing opportunities when they present themselves. No one in the world of commerce gave the Koreans anything. Instead, zeal to achieve led Koreans and their companies to strive to demonstrate their worth and earn respect through competitive success.

5 CORPORATE STRATEGY AND GLOBAL COMPETITION

Korean Air is not only the flagship air carrier of the Republic of Korea and the official airline of the 1988 Seoul Olympics; it is also the second-largest airline in Asia and the pride of the Hanjin Group. Flying to twenty-eight major cities in seventeen countries and serving over 7 million passengers a year, Korean Air is big by any standard of comparison. Its owner, Hanjin, was founded in 1945 and is Korea's ninth-largest chaebol group with sales over $3 billion. (The group is also involved in sea and land transportation, banking and insurance, construction and realty, and even runs a university.) With close government ties and driving ambition, Korean Air and Hanjin, under the direction of a committed entrepreneur named Cho Choong Hoon, continue to grow and prosper. Their motto is "Enterprise is a form of art."

Yet Korean Air is now facing something it has not seen before on its domestic routes: competition. To open its markets to increased competition, the Korean government has allowed the establishment of a second airline, first for domestic service and later for international routes. Despite competition from such major groups as Samsung, the award went to the Kumho Group, a relatively small yet tenacious company considered by many to be Korea's most profitable chaebol (Kim and Shim 1988). Beginning in 1989 Kumho began flying domestic air routes with its new Asiana Airlines.

71

The Kumho Group, begun in 1946, started its existence as a taxi company. Soon it expanded into bus transportation, then tires, synthetic rubber, and chemicals. In 1974 the current chairman, Park Seong Yawng, assumed control from his father, the founder of Kumho. Park, a Yale Ph.D. in economics, wanted to be a teacher and initially accepted a position at the University of California, Berkeley. However, after two years, Korean President Park Chung Hee asked him to return to Korea as the president's economic secretary. When released from this commitment, Professor Park returned to teaching at Sogang University in Seoul. However, his academic career was again short-lived. With his father's illness, the Kumho Group needed him, and he accepted the challenge—and responsibility. He set about the task of building the company into a large conglomerate, including electronics, steel, and financial services. When we interviewed Chairman Park in 1988, he indicated that the move into the airline industry was simply a logical extension for a company long concerned with transportation. "Our people work hard," Park noted, "and we are committed to building Kumho into a major player in the air transportation industry."

At home and abroad, both Hanjin and Kumho have approached corporate strategy and competition with renewed vigor. In fact, as most Korean corporations face an increasingly free marketplace with fewer government-imposed restrictions, subsidies, and monopolies, the concept of corporate strategy is becoming a much more salient organizational variable. This chapter examines how Korean companies approach strategy and global competition as they attempt to capture an ever-increasing share of the global marketplace. First the concept of strategy is examined to provide a reference for the analysis that follows.

COMPETITIVE STRATEGY:
A FRAMEWORK FOR ANALYSIS

Broadly defined, *strategy* refers to an interlocking pattern of decisions designed to create a sustainable competitive advantage for a firm. In assessing a firm's strategy, two questions are generally raised: (1) How effectively is the firm strategically positioned in the industry? and (2) How can the firm sustain its competitive advantage over time? Poor positioning within the industry can lead to lower rates of return relative to competitors. On the other hand, good positioning can lead to high rates of return, even if the industry structure is unattractive. Without a sustainable competitive advantage, a firm is likely to lose its market position and ultimately become unprofitable.

In his seminal book entitled *Competitive Strategy*, Michael Porter defined three "generic strategies" by which a firm can achieve a competitive advantage in an industry: (1) cost leadership, (2) product differentiation, and (3) focus or market niche (Porter 1980). In a *cost leadership* strategy, a firm attempts to become the lowest-cost producer in the industry. This is typically achieved with economies of scale, proprietary technology, preferred raw material access, and automation. IBM is often identified as a low cost leader in mainframe computers, enabling it to enter most major computer markets almost at will. In contrast, in the *product differentiation* strategy a firm attempts to become unique along some nonprice dimension that is valued by buyers in the industry. Typically, this would involve differentiation by service, product performance, capability, technology, or product distribution. Apple Computers is sometimes contrasted with IBM in that it constantly differentiates its features, enabling it to set higher prices for its personal computers. Finally, in the *focus* or *niche* strategy, a firm selects a market niche and tailors its strategy to serving this niche more so than others. A focused firm such as Tandy Computers attempts to service the particular or proprietary needs of this segment that might not be well served by the broad line of producers.

When these models are put into practice among multinational firms, a major issue emerges concerning whether the firm should strive to be the innovator or the "first mover" or should deliberately wait for a leader to emerge and build a market before imitating or improving on the leader's products. It was traditionally believed that leaders held the key to worldwide penetration and dominance, particularly when they are able to successfully build an advantage in their domestic markets through cost leadership or product differentiation. In such cases, extending dominance to overseas markets would be relatively easy because followers would not be able to overcome the first-mover advantage developed by the innovator. Buyers, already satisfied with the performance of the innovator, might forgo the costs of obtaining information on lesser-known imitators. Moreover, innovators, by building volume rapidly, could maintain a significant cost advantage over the followers on the experience curve. According to this model, the goal was to be first to market. However, as popular as this theory has been with a wide array of managers and teachers of management, it does not provide an accurate picture of how the Koreans—and the Japanese before them—achieved market success.

KOREA VERSUS JAPAN IN GLOBAL COMPETITION

Much has been written over the years about the success of the Japanese in global competition, and now similar articles are appearing about Korea. A central theme of many of these pieces is the similarity between the Japanese and Korean approaches to strategy. In his recent book entitled *Is Korea the Next Japan?*, T. W. Kang (1989) argues that although similarities can clearly be found between the approaches taken by the two countries, important differences must also be noted. Our own interviews with executives, scholars, and government officials reinforce this conclusion. The Korean approach to strategy is in many ways quite different from the approach typically taken by Japanese concerns. To appreciate these differences, it is first necessary to understand the situation in Japan during the early stages of its economic development.

The Japanese Approach to Strategy

In his 1982 book *The Mind of the Strategist*, Kenichi Ohmae succinctly described the Japanese competitive strategy as evolving through three basic phases: (1) Enter at the lower end, (2) expand to medium and high ends, and (3) "win the world." Entering at the low end implies that Japanese firms were able to effectively penetrate a given market at a price that was lower than that of the industry leader. This often occurs at the start of a mature market, when industry incumbents are no longer able to effectively differentiate their products (such as color televisions, steel, and consumer electronics) through advertising or process engineering. For this strategy to be successful, the new entrant (the Japanese company) has to be the cost-leader or have the lowest costs among competitors in the industry (Abegglen and Stalk 1985).

There are several reasons why the Japanese have been able to enter a market late and still have a competitive edge over the other companies in the field. For instance, Japanese firms typically enjoy the benefits of lower costs of capital, lower information and transactional costs, and lower personnel-related costs that follow from a stable, committed, and well-trained workforce. Unlike their American counterparts, which are continually under pressure to show profits on a quarterly basis, Japanese firms can afford to invest massive sums into process engineering and automation to reduce their overall costs. Indeed, because labor costs are treated as fixed costs under a lifetime employment system, a strategy of productivity increases that reduce overall costs through improved manufacturing processes represents the optimal course of action. Operating in a domestic market that is initially closed to foreign competitors and much more competitive than most export markets, Japanese firms are able to move down the experience curve at a rapid rate, thereby accelerating the maturity of products that they target for world penetration.

The Korean Approach to Strategy

Although many similarities exist between the typical Korean approach to corporate strategy and that of the Japanese, Korea is not a second Japan. Korean companies do, in fact, make it a practice to enter an international market late as an aggressive cost leader, like their Japanese counterparts. Indeed, it is somewhat ironic that the Koreans are now successfully challenging the Japanese—the very architects of the highly regarded delayed entry strategy—in the global marketplace. Several Japanese electronics firms have recently expressed frustration at the recent successes of Korean companies like Goldstar, Daewoo, and Samsung in the home appliance and electronics export markets. For instance, Korean-made VCRs now account for over 20 percent of all VCRs exported to the United States, compared to only 3 percent just four years ago. Korea also is entering other markets previously dominated by the Japanese, such as automobiles, dynamic random access memory (DRAM) semiconductors, and personal computers. It is no wonder that some Japanese have confided that the Koreans are "accelerating their timetable for easing out mature products"—the same tactic that the Japanese had successfully deployed against U.S. and European competitors (Ungson 1990).

However, in explaining *how* Koreans have achieved their cost leadership position, significant differences between the Japanese and Korean approaches emerge. Compared to the Japanese, Koreans do not have an extensive domestic market to develop economies of scale. Nor do they have Japan's wide array of nontariff trade barriers to protect against foreign competitors. Although a domestic market is beginning to develop and trade barriers are clearly present, they are not as extensive or sophisticated as those found in Japan during the developmental stage of a market. In addition, Koreans do not have as large a personal saving rate as the Japanese do and hence do not enjoy the advantages of a lower cost of capital. Finally, Koreans have been largely dependent on foreign competitors for new technologies. Hyundai's entry into the automotive market would not have been possible without the early assistance of Mitsubishi, and most Korean VCRs contain numerous components from Japanese electronics firms. Although this situation is beginning to change, it is a strategic limitation facing most Korean companies, which must develop their own approach to international competition.

How, then, do Korean companies succeed? In an interview with Lee Hong Kyu, deputy minister of the Industrial Policy Division at Korea's Ministry of Trade and Industry (KMTI), two main factors were suggested to help explain Korea's global success. First, the nation's industrial policy has focused on aggressive export promotion, combined with a myriad of export incentives, selective import liberalizations, directed credit, and various export instruments (see Chapter 2). Coupled with generous loans to selected companies, the policy has enabled the Koreans to develop the infrastructure necessary for their cost leadership strategy. From a national perspective, this strategy has clearly paid off with respect to trade with Western nations such as the United States, and the Koreans hope it will soon reap benefits in their trade with Japan (see Exhibit 5–1).

Second, there has been an effort to maximize the efficiency of corporations' human resources (see Chapter 7). Korea's distinctive advantage, not unknown to its major competitors, is a highly educated, motivated, and relatively inexpensive labor force. Indeed, in private, some Korean corporate officials we talked with faulted U.S. workers for having "questionable" work habits and for lacking the

Exhibit 5-1. 1987 Korean Imports from and Exports to the United States and Japan.*

	United States	*Japan*
Imports from:	*$8 billion*	*$13 billion*
	Machinery and transport equipment (34%)	Manufactures and machinery (59%)
	Raw materials (32%)	Chemicals (13%)
	Chemicals (13%)	Metals (12%)
	Food (9%)	Textile and clothing (5%)
	Manufactured goods (6%)	Raw materials (2%)
	Other (6%)	Other (9%)
Exports to:	*$18 billion*	*$8 billion*
	Textiles and footwear (29%)	Textiles (27%)
	Electrical equipment (21%)	Food (18%)
	Manufactures and machinery (20%)	Machinery and transport equipment (13%)
	Autos (12%)	Steel (10%)
	Toys (6%)	Chemicals (5%)
	Food (2%)	Fuels (5%)
	Chemicals (1%)	Raw materials (3%)
	Other (9%)	Other (19%)

*Percentages reflect amount of total imports or exports per category as a percentage of total imports or exports.

Source: Data based on U.S. Department of Commerce and Japanese Ministry of International Trade and Industry as compiled by *The Economist*, 21 May 1988, 15-22.

hunger and drive to succeed. It is referred to quietly as the "American disease." Hence, a combination of guided export support programs and efficient human resource management emerge as primary factors aiding Korea's drive for success.

Additional insight on this issue was provided in an interview with Dr. Park Ungsuh, executive vice president of Samsung Co., Ltd. After describing Samsung's early years competing against other Korean firms, Dr. Park said a decision was made in the 1970s that the company had to begin competing on a worldwide basis. Looking to the immediate future, Park noted, "We are the world assemblers of mature products and we aim to be bigger in large-scale production than anyone else." In competition where size is a critical component,

Koreans have decided to exploit their advantage to the fullest extent possible. With a relatively small domestic market, they correctly assumed that their lower-priced products would be competitive virtually anywhere in the world. It was an aggressive statement that described not only Samsung's strategic intent but also that of Goldstar, Hyundai, Pohang Steel, and other successful Korean multinationals.

Exhibit 5-2 depicts the typical pattern of Korean market entry strategies as compared to Korea's international competitors. As can be seen in the case of the world television industry, Korea entered the market much later than the United States and Japan. The television sector was targeted for special government assistance in the late 1960s with the enactment of the Promotion of Electronics Industry law, which provided the Korean television industry with government assistance and access to foreign capital and technology. By 1972 five Korean companies were producing black-and-white sets that were developed from Japanese licensed technology. With aggressive export promotion and pricing, the Koreans were able to secure contracts with K-Mart and Sears (Yoffie and Salorio 1986).

The entry into color televisions proved to be formidable. Permission to use Japanese-license rights came after years of tense negotiations, and when Korean companies built capacity to produce color televisions far in excess of sales, the U.S. and Korean governments agreed to restrict sales of Korean color televisions in the United States. Fortunately, color broadcasting in Korea started in 1979, and sales to Korea's domestic market alleviated this problem. In 1982 exports to the United States soared, making Korea the third-largest producer of color televisions. Eventually three Korean TV manufacturers started assembly facilities in the United States.

Korea's success in both black-and-white and color television sets was premised on becoming the low-cost producer in the industry. Korean manufacturers kept their prices 10 to 15 percent lower than competitors anywhere they marketed. To meet their goal of mass distribution, they used both traditional outlets (independent dealers and large multiple outlets) and other novel channels such as supermarkets and pharmacies. In large measure, Korean sets were sold as OEM or as private labels. The Koreans were particularly adept in competing in the low end of the market that favored their low-cost position. By 1983, when export restrictions were lifted in the United States, Korea had become the major source of U.S. color televisions, surpassing both Taiwan and Japan.

Exhibit 5–2. Television Exports from Korea, Japan, and the United States, 1963–81.

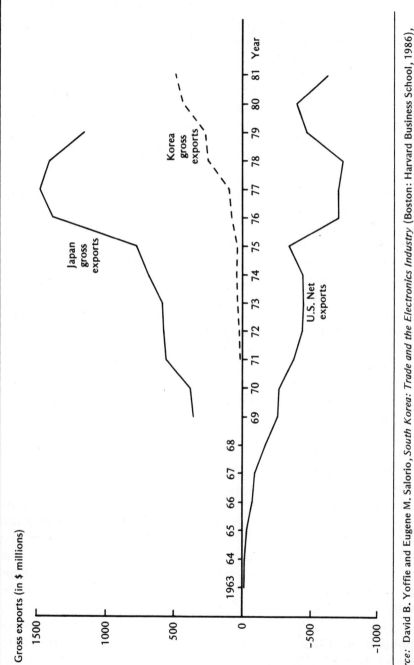

Source: David B. Yoffie and Eugene M. Salorio, *South Korea: Trade and the Electronics Industry* (Boston: Harvard Business School, 1986), case 387–036. Reprinted by permission.

EXAMPLES OF SUCCESSFUL
STRATEGIC IMPLEMENTATION

The success of Korea's cost leadership strategy is a result of many interlocking factors: an aggressive industrial policy directed at export promotion, institutional support and incentives for export-oriented companies, lower wages relative to competitors, economies of scale derived from very large-scale manufacturing facilities, institutionalized entrepreneurship, a highly educated and motivated labor force, and corporate skills and adeptness at reverse-engineering, or what Samsung's Dr. Park refers to as "value-added engineering" (that is, an ability to adapt complex foreign technology into forms that are simpler to produce).

Two examples illustrate the success of this strategy in the international marketplace. First, we examine Samsung's entry into the household appliance market, specifically in microwave ovens. Next, since there is emerging evidence that the traditional Korean entry strategy may be changing in order to meet the new demands of global competition, we examine how the big four chaebols entered the worldwide semiconductor market.

Global Competition in
Microwave Ovens

It has been described as the "microwave war," but only a few years ago it would have hardly qualified as a contest (Magaziner and Patinkin 1989). The microwave oven, invented in the United States by Raytheon engineers in 1949, rapidly emerged as yet another Japanese consumer electronics product. Several American companies manufactured it, but most discovered that they could not compete against the production efficiency established by Japanese concerns. At the same time, however, and ignored by both the Americans and the Japanese, engineers at Samsung's sprawling Suwon complex prepared to do battle with their formidable competitors.

Samsung's decision to enter the microwave oven market came after a visit by Samsung Vice President J. U. Chung to the United States in 1976. During the visit, Chung became fascinated by the microwave oven and concluded that it offered his company a good opportunity. In making this decision, however, Samsung faced monumental obstacles—enough to discourage any world-class competitor. The product could not be marketed in Korea because few Koreans could afford to pay for it. Moreover, both the Japanese (led by Matsushita and Sanyo) and several U.S. manufacturers (like General Electric) had already taken a commanding lead in the market. But Samsung was not discouraged. After all, the company had built its reputation as a relentless innovator in manufacturing technology. At a time when there was not a single television station in Korea, Samsung had assembled color television sets for companies from all over the world—including RCA, GE, and Hitachi—and had proudly assembled their very own.

The legacy of Samsung's engineering talent started with Samsung's Chairman Lee Byung Chull, who believed that investment in people's minds was as good as any investment in technology. Under his tutelage, Samsung had built the largest engineering pool in any developing country. When Chu Yun Soo was given the assignment to design and produce Samsung's first microwave oven, he eschewed the normal arguments that Korea was too far behind to succeed; in fact, he immediately ordered the Jet 230, a new microwave oven made by General Electric. When it arrived, Chu discovered his first major problem: the technology of the microwave rested on the magnetron tube, something that required expertise the company did not have. Even so, Samsung gave Chu and his group a ringing endorsement: "Don't worry about selling the item—learn how to produce it first."

Chu selected the best models to develop his own prototype. He improvised in its development, substituting caulking to seal the oven when he could not find the necessary welding equipment. The problematic magnetron tube had to be secured from the Japanese—a task made easy by the fact that the Japanese and Americans were now producing over 4 million units per year. When Chu tested the first prototype in June 1978, it failed. Nonetheless, Samsung encouraged him to continue and even commissioned a makeshift production line. By mid-1979, when Samsung had finally solved their technical problems and had manufactured a mere 1,460 units, over 5 million had been sold all over the world by Japanese and American manufacturers. Even so, Samsung had every reason to celebrate: They had finally succeeded in manufactured a commercially viable product and had obtained their first order from Panama. Of course, the sale was made at a financial loss to Samsung.

Samsung's first break in the market came when J. C. Penney began searching for a less expensive model to market under their own brand name. Getting little satisfaction from the Japanese and American manufacturers, J. C. Penney selected Samsung and commissioned a microwave oven to be sold for $299 in the United States. Under the leadership of Chu's boss, Park Kyung Pal, product and manufacturing teams were forged together with one unbendable rule: no matter what, it would meet deadlines. Samsung lost money on the venture, but J. C. Penney liked the initial product and ordered several thousand more. The deadline was again met. In another month, the order had risen to 7,000. Samsung was in the microwave oven market.

Samsung's second break occurred when General Electric appliances began losing market share to the Japanese. Suspecting that the Japanese were dumping, GE asked a management consultant, Ira Magaziner, to do a study. The study concluded that there was no evidence of dumping; GE was simply not cost competitive. In his report, Magaziner suggested that the American company consider producing the ovens overseas, possibly in Korea. After Matsushita declined a proposed joint venture arrangement, attention shifted to Samsung. After some initial skepticism, GE relented and gave Samsung a small order—only 15,000 ovens. Even then, there was doubt whether the Koreans could deliver a high-quality product to the U.S. market. But Samsung set about its task. At first, Samsung's ovens failed to meet GE's demanding standards, but things eventually improved. Throughout, Samsung repeatedly astonished the Americans with an increasing array of improvements in their manufacturing plants and systems. By the end of 1984 Samsung's production had reached 1 million units. The alliance between Samsung and GE prospered: General Electric had provided the scale to make Samsung a world-class competitor in household appliances and in exchange had received a successful product for the American market. Both are now targeting the lucrative European market. While GE attempts to leverage its prominent retailing position overseas, Samsung sees itself as possibly emerging as the next GE.

Entry into High-Technology Markets:
The Case of Semiconductors

Critics of the Korean miracle frequently note that Korean companies tend to succeed in maturing markets or with products that have reached commodity status in Japan, the United States, and Europe. This is said to account for their ability to enter markets at a late stage and yet compete as cost leaders. However, the question remains whether Koreans can achieve a similar miracle in fast-growing, embryonic high-technology industries such as microelectronics, computers, and telecommunications.

There are several reasons why a competitive presence in high technology is desired if not essential for Korean firms. High-technology industries represent the fastest-growing economic sector in the United States over the last two decades. For example, the U.S. semiconductor industry had a compounded annual growth rate of 33 percent from 1972 to 1986 (Ungson 1990). Dubbed the "crude oil of the 1990s" by some Americans and the "rice of the high-technology industry" by Samsung founder B. C. Lee, semiconductors have made possible a variety of new applications for products and markets that have led to rapid growth in such fields as computers, connectors, instruments, agricultural machinery, electronic banking, satellite-based telecommunications, consumer electronics, and consumer products.

Beyond the rapid rate of growth, most high-technology sectors (particularly microelectronics) also qualify as global industries. Porter (1985) has identified several factors that have accelerated the globalization of industries, including the growing similarity of consumer tastes around the world, more fluid capital markets, falling tariff barriers, and the homogenizing effects of technology. The implication for international competitors is clear: either become a full-fledged global competitor or become a second-rate player in the process. A belief that is becoming entrenched is that leadership in high technology is the key to global economic leadership in the decades to come. Certainly, Korea aspires to become a global competitor, but to do so it has to join the ranks of established leaders such as the United States, Japan, and the EEC, as well as the newly industrializing countries (such as Taiwan, Singapore, and Hong Kong) that have elected to compete in high-technology battle.

How well can Korea compete in high technology? In discussions with T. G. Kim, executive vice president of Daewoo's Planning and Coordination Division, and Dr. Park Sung Kyou, president of Daewoo Telecom (the Korean partner in the successful Leading Edge microcomputer venture), both pointed to the enormous difficulty of framing Korea's new corporate strategy in high technology. Dr. Park suggested that Koreans have to overcome two primary problems in order to compete effectively: Korea's relative lack of skilled engineers and its dependence on the United States and Japan for new technologies.

To resolve these problems Daewoo and other companies strive to recruit large numbers of engineers and scientists, which is no easy task. Each year, Korean universities graduate approximately 4,500 electrical engineers. About 1,500 of the very best go abroad for advanced training, leaving only 3,000 engineers to satisfy all the companies in the market. (Samsung alone claims that it could use all 3,000.) As a result of this personnel shortage, many firms have gone abroad in an attempt to recruit overseas Koreans who are willing to return home and work at high levels in the Korean firms. This repatriation effort has provided returning engineers with significant financial and job-related inducements and has met with considerable success (Kang 1989). In fact, several of the executives we interviewed were repatriated Koreans.

In addition, companies attempting to meet the high-tech challenge work to acquire necessary technology either through licensing or through joint ventures with foreign firms. The use of joint ventures in the electronics field can be seen in several examples. For instance, Lucky-Goldstar has numerous joint ventures for its various electronic-related subsidiaries, including Goldstar Cable Company with Hitachi, Goldstar Tele-Electric with Siemens, Goldstar Electric with NEC, Goldstar Instrument and Electric with Fuji Electric, Goldstar Semiconductor with AT&T, Goldstar Alps with Alps Electric, Goldstar Honeywell with Honeywell-Bull, and Shinyeong Elevator with Mitsubishi. Similarly, Samsung companies have joint ventures with such foreign firms as NEC, Sumitomo, Corning, Hewlett-Packard, General Dynamics, Sikorsky, and General Electric.

Finally, companies pursuing a high-tech agenda invest significant amounts of money in research and development in order to catch up with foreign competitors. This is illustrated in the graph shown in Exhibit 5-3, which traces aggregate investments in R&D from 1977 to 1986. Particularly interesting here is the rather startling increase in expenditures for research over the past several years. Indeed, several Korean companies appear not to be content with matching the competition; they intend to surpass it.

To see how these efforts come together for purposes of international competition, consider the example of Korea's entry into the semiconductor market. In 1974 Korea had no chip manufacturing

Exhibit 5-3. Increases in R&D Investments by Korean Firms, 1977–86.

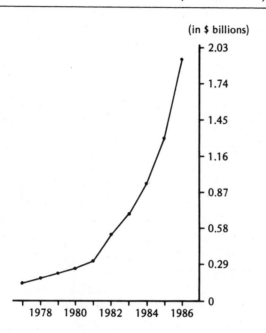

Source: Based on information from the Korean Ministry of Science and Technology as reported in *The Economist*, 21 May, 1988, pp. 4–20.

facilities, and the semiconductor business was controlled by the United States and Japan. The market for semiconductors was bound to increase, not just for computers but also for high-definition television, enhanced VCRs, intelligent fax machines, and new-model cellular phones. In fact, the market for memory chips was $50 billion in 1988 (*The Economist* 1989). Clearly this was a business the major chaebols wanted to be involved in.

First into the market was Samsung in 1974, followed closely by Lucky-Goldstar in 1979. By 1983 Hyundai and Daewoo had entered the business. With technology borrowed from the United States and Japan, these four companies intended not just to participate in the market but to dominate it by the end of the 1980s. The 1985 recession, which drove many U.S. firms out of the memory chip business, failed to deter the Koreans. Samsung alone invested over $523 million on chip research between 1985 and 1987, and the results were dramatic (see Exhibit 5–4). By 1988 the big four chaebols sold over

Exhibit 5-4.   Sales of Korean Semiconductors, 1984–88.

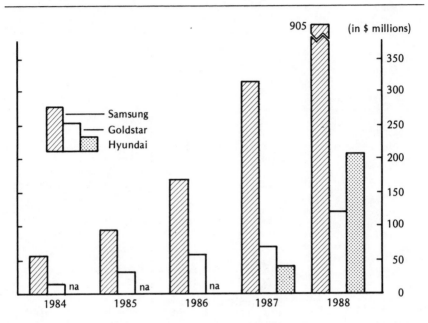

$1.2 billion worth of chips, and in 1989 this figure promises to be 20 to 30 percent higher.

These companies are now beginning to go up-market. Samsung, Lucky-Goldstar, and Hyundai are all capable of manufacturing the newer 1MB DRAM chip, designed for the latest computers and HDTV. By 1988 people in the business began to realize how quickly the Korean firms were catching up with their Japanese and American competitors. *Dataquest,* an industry analyst, observed that this technology gap had narrowed from thirty years in 1975 to two or three years in 1986 and would virtually close by 1990. In the mid-1980s, in an effort to help close this gap, the government invested $100 million in a consortium of companies to develop the 4MB DRAM chip by 1990. The program ended early: Samsung had developed a prototype by February 1988.

It is clear, then, that Korean firms have been reasonably successful in adopting strategies that made use of their strengths and proved beneficial over the long run. We should hasten to point out, however, that success is not always ensured. Hyundai, for example, attempted three times to enter the U.S. microelectronics market. The first venture, Hyundai Electronics of America (HEA) failed with a loss estimated to be $40 million. The second venture involved marketing its own microcomputers in partnership with an American firm under the brand name Blue Chip. This venture also failed. However, learning from its mistakes, Hyundai now markets its microcomputers in the United States under its own name, and the effort to date has proven successful.

The next strategic horizon for successful Korean firms involves expansion overseas. Whether motivated by lower labor costs for manufacturing (as can be found in Thailand, China, and the Philippines), a desire to be closer to their markets or protect themselves from tariff restrictions (as in North America and Europe), or simply a chance to capitalize on unique investment opportunities (many firms are currently investing in California real estate), Korean firms are spending more overseas. In fact, overseas investment has risen from $57 million in 1984 to $213 in 1988—a fourfold increase in just five years—and 1989-90 will prove even larger (Clifford and Moore 1989).

At home and abroad, the executives of the major chaebol groups have learned the lessons of competitive strategy and global competition. Based on these strategies, their next challenge is how to facilitate attaining these strategic objectives in an efficient and effective manner. This is the domain of organization design and management process, and it is to this topic that we now turn.

6 ORGANIZATION DESIGN AND THE WORK ENVIRONMENT

In his award-winning book, *The Reckoning* (1986), David Halber-stram tells the story of Park Jin Kean, a foreman at the Hyundai motor works in Ulsan. Like many Koreans, Park left a farming village to enter the industrial world because he felt it had greater promise for the future. He moved to Ulsan (200 miles southeast of Seoul) in 1974 and applied along with 400 others for the 50 blue-collar jobs that were open. Despite being nervous during the selection interview and giving what he thought were wrong answers to several questions (such as "If something bad happens inside the company, would you tell anyone from the outside?"), he got the job.

In the early days the work was hard. The assembly line was not automated, and the workers were inexperienced. The parts made by suppliers were of poor quality, and the men had little idea of what they were doing. Park remembers that the assembly-line usually worked about 20 to 30 percent of the time and that a shift could produce about twenty cars per day. Park knew that the cars were not very good, but like the other workers, he was told by his supervisor that things would improve and that it was his obligation to persevere. He did, and slowly the situation got better. Hyundai Motors exchanged 15 percent of its stock with Mitsubishi for technical assistance and training. (It is said that other Japanese auto companies were angry at Mitsubishi for sharing this knowledge with "these upstart Koreans.") Gradually, the workers at Hyundai came to understand what was expected of them. Their technical knowledge improved, as did the quality of parts from suppliers.

The critical year was 1979. Before this, the company had achieved a level of production of one car every four minutes and thirty-eight seconds. As the technical assistance began to come together and a semi-automated assembly line was put in place, production surged to one car every two minutes. The work pace was exhausting, but Park never complained. He worked twelve hours a day, six days a week. He had no effective union representation. Still, living with his wife and two children in a small company-owned high-rise apartment near the factory, he was convinced that his new life in the industrial world was far better than that of his parents on the farm.

After seven years on the assembly line, Park was promoted to foreman. He is proud of his job and fiercely loyal to the company, and his 1986 salary of $9,600 was much higher than that of the average Korean, who made $2,000 per year. The company too has done well. In 1981 Hyundai produced only 60,000 cars of dubious quality. By 1986 this figure had risen to more than 400,000 cars of fine quality, and the company was hoping to produce 1 million by 1990. As Park sits back and looks at the new employees now entering Hyundai, he wonders if they are perhaps too intense. A sign has been posted on the factory walls asking workers not to rush their jobs but to take the time to ensure a high-quality product. As he considers the drive and dedication of these younger workers, he and his colleagues jokingly refer to the Japanese as "the lazy Asians."

ORGANIZATION AND MANAGEMENT

In Chapter 3, several macro-design issues of Korean corporations were considered, including the role of the central office of the chairman and the divisional structure of several of the major groups. This chapter continues this analysis by looking inside a typical Korean corporation at structural issues such as employee groupings and the organization of such groupings within a company as they affect management practice, the major factors that characterize a typical work environment, and management practices of Korean firms operating manufacturing facilities in the United States.

Employee Groupings

A good place to begin an analysis of organization design is with the categorization of employees within a company. In general, Korean companies consist of three categories of employees: a core group, a middle or regular group, and a marginal group (Shin 1988c). The *core* group consists of essential employees who are usually long-term employees (and owners) who have chosen to tie their fate to that of the organization. These individuals are highly valued by the chairman and are typically treated well. The basic, or *regular*, group consists of rank-and-file employees (both managers and workers) who have worked for the company for a sufficient time to build some commitments on both sides. Some regular employees advance to become part of the core group, while others leave voluntarily or involuntarily and go to other enterprises. (Members of the core group seldom leave.) Although lifetime employment as a policy is not as strong in Korea as it is in Japan, mutual commitments and an expanding economy have minimized major dislocations among this group. The final group, *marginal* employees, are often hired through personal contacts or connections. These people often lack the typical high motivation level but usually are not laid off during economic downturns because of their connections.

To help understand this triple stratum grouping, it may be helpful to compare Korea to Japan and the United States (see Exhibit 6-1). In Japan, a double-stratum system is typical. This consists of a somewhat larger core group than normally found in Korea—and to whom lifetime employment is granted—and a middle or regular group (including women) that experiences less mutual commitment but nevertheless enjoys relatively stable employment. As in Korea, the core group is primarily responsible for preserving and developing the company and, as such, is considered part of the corporate family. It has been estimated that the ratio of employees for the three groups in Korea is about 10:80:10 and that in Japan the ratio is about 30:70 (Shin 1988c).

In American companies, by contrast, very few people are considered "core" employees. That is, with few exceptions, American companies consider most people—even managers near the top—to be employees and not members of a corporate family. Despite the rhetoric, most top executives of U.S. firms feel that employees are

Exhibit 6-1. Employee Groupings in Korea, Japan and the United States.

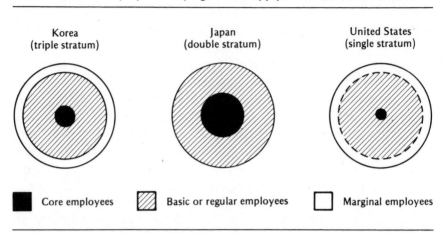

| Korea (triple stratum) | Japan (double stratum) | United States (single stratum) |

■ Core employees   ▨ Basic or regular employees   □ Marginal employees

Source: Yoo Keun Shin, "Human Resources Management in Korea," paper presented at the Tenth International Conference of the Korean Personnel Management Association, Seoul, 21 May 1988.

expendable, and they seldom display the mutual or two-way commitments found in Korea and Japan. Hence, the typical U.S. firm can be described as a single-stratum organization, with a very thin core (often the owners) and a large regular employee cluster. Managers and workers within this cluster may have differing employment contracts and differing outlooks, but the two groups nonetheless share the common characteristic of being employees and not family. Moreover, some of these employees may be considered temporary in the sense that they may be laid off during poor business conditions. For all practical purposes, however, they constitute one rather large group.

Organizational Structure

Beyond these employee groupings, it is interesting to examine how various employee groups are organized for purposes of management. Here, with some exceptions, the Korean and American models are similar. A typical organizational hierarchy for a Korean firm is shown in Exhibit 6-2. Three principal groupings can be noted: managers and technical personnel, workers, and female employees. As in the United

Exhibit 6-2. Typical Organizational Hierarchy for a Korean Firm.

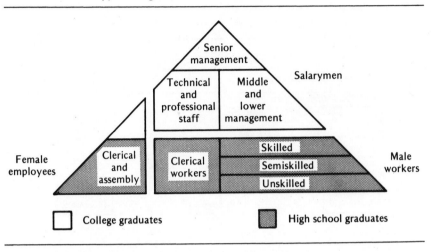

States, a dual-track hierarchy among white-collar employees can be found, consisting of a managerial and a technical track. These people are referred to as *salarymen* in both Korea and Japan and invariably consist of college graduates who entered the company through a very rigorous selection procedure (see Chapter 7).

Below this can be found the blue-collar workers, divided (as in the United States) into skilled, semi-skilled, and unskilled workers. This is the group that Park entered at Hyundai. As seen in the Park example, these workers typically exhibit a commitment level toward the organization that far exceeds that of their American or European counterparts. Even during labor troubles (when goal conflicts are clearly evident—see Chapter 7), their commitment to the company is seldom challenged.

The Hyundai Motor Company where Park works offers a good example of how a production unit is organized (K. Bae, 1987; K. Bae and Form 1986). Employees are required to have their hair cut short and wear the grey company uniform. Employee rank is identified by the shape of the name tags that are attached to the left breast pocket. The organization of a production unit in the Hyundai factory is shown in Exhibit 6-3. As can be seen, six to ten production workers (or *kongwon*) are supervised by a foreman (*chojang*). Twenty to forty *kongwon* with their three *chojang* report to a supervisor (*banjang*) who, along with two or three other *banjang* report to a

Exhibit 6-3.   Organization Chart for a Production Unit at
Hyundai Motor Company.

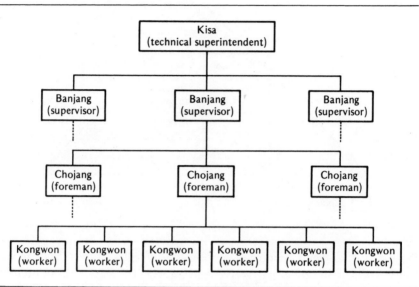

Source: Based on information reported by K. Bae, *Automobile Workers in Korea* (Seoul: Seoul National University Press, 1987), and K. Bae and W. Form, "Payment Strategy in South Korea's Advanced Economic Sector," *American Sociological Review* (February 1986): 120–31.

technical superintendent, or *kisa.* In this highly centralized arrangement, the first two levels of supervision are almost horizontal in that their occupants work on the production line. All three levels of supervision cooperate in evaluating individual worker performance.

Finally, the place of female employees in corporations is perhaps best understood as consisting of a separate hierarchy, totally distinct from and largely subservient to the male hierarchy. This practice follows from Confucian tradition and results in a situation where women are paid less, have less job security, and are allowed little input into the decisionmaking process. Women are hired almost exclusively as assemblers, clerks, typists, secretaries, or service workers. Female college graduates earn more and have somewhat higher status and authority (see Exhibit 6-2), but they like other women are clearly less important to the organization than are the salarymen or workers and earn less than males doing similar jobs. They are seen as temporary employees whose role is to serve the (male) organization until marriage. Although changes in the status of women in Korea have been slow to come, some evolution is discernible. For example, Daewoo recently began hiring former female employees on a part-time basis when their children were largely grown. (The role of women in the corporation is returned to later in this chapter.)

THE WORK ENVIRONMENT

At the risk of overgeneralizing, it is possible to develop a composite picture of a typical work environment in a Korean company by observing central tendencies across companies. (Of course, variations on these tendencies and exceptions to the trends can be found.) If this is done, seven predominant characteristics emerge that help explain the Korean approach to management, production, research, and the marketplace: (1) the Korean work ethic, (2) group harmony and the social contract, (3) basis for career success, (4) paternalism in superior-subordinate relationships, (5) importance of personal relationships, (6) decisionmaking processes, and (7) the role of women in the workplace. Most Korean corporations have created a work environment that is consistent with Korean societal norms and that is highly conducive to maximum production and maximum effort on behalf of the goals of the corporation.

Korean Work Ethic

Simply put, the Korean work ethic is legendary. Foreign observers frequently describe Korean workers as diligent, self-sacrificing, dedicated, and dependable. Even the Japanese complain that the Koreans work too hard. Consider, for example, company slogans like Daewoo's "Creativity, challenge, and sacrifice." Or consider a recent survey that asked school children from several countries what important values their parents would like to see in them. Results showed that achievement ranked number one among Korean children and ranked sixth and eight among English and American children (Wright 1987). Finally, in a study done by Kim Kyong-Dong (1985), Korean managers were asked what they would do if they had enough money to live comfortably for the remainder of their lives. A full 96 percent responded that they would continue to work hard despite their new wealth. Asked if the managers would prefer to have more time for work or for leisure, 61 percent responded that they would prefer to have more time for work, and only 38 percent said they would prefer more leisure time.

Another way to examine the work ethic is to consider actual behavioral manifestations of it. For example, the average male industrial worker works an average of 53.8 hours per week, reportedly the longest work week in the world (*Business Korea* 1986, 26); women work somewhat less than this. It is estimated that the average Korean works a total of 2,833 hours per year for males, compared to 2,168 hours in Japan, 1,898 in the United States, or 1,652 in West Germany (see Exhibit 6-4). Similarly, although entitled to more, the average Korean actually takes 4.5 days vacation per year, compared to 9.6 in Japan, 19.5 in the United States, or 30.2 in West Germany (Japanese Ministry of Labor 1986; Kang 1989).

Exhibit 6-5 shows the working hours for Park's Hyundai Motor Company in Ulsan (K. Bae 1987). As can be seen, the average assembly-line worker works twelve hours per day, at least six days per week (and sometimes on Sunday depending on production demands). Female workers typically work about nine hours per day and usually leave work around 6:00 P.M. to return home to help the family with dinner. Finally, salarymen are usually at work around twelve to fourteen hours per day, six days per week. However, this includes several hours per night after dinner socializing with their

Exhibit 6-4. Average Hours Worked Per Year and Vacation Taken for Male Industrial Workers.

	Average Hours Worked Per Year	Vacation Days Actually Taken
Korea	2,833	4.5
Japan	2,180	9.6
United States	1,934	19.5
Great Britain	1,941	22.5
West Germany	1,652	30.2
France	1,649	25.0

Source: Based on data reported by Japanese Ministry of Labor, "The Japanese Work Week," white paper (Japanese Ministry of Labor: Tokyo, 1986); "Womanpower: Unsung Praises," *Business Korea*, September 1986, 20-25; and T. W. Kang, *Is Korea the Next Japan?* (New York: Free Press, 1989).

Exhibit 6–5. Working Hours at Hyundai Motor Company: Monday through Saturday.

Time	Manufacturing Workers*	Salarymen	Female Employees
08:00–10:00			
Break			
10:10–12:00			
Lunch			
13:00–15:00			
Break			
15:10–17:00			
Dinner			
18:00–20:00			
Break			
20:10–22:00			
Tea and cookies			
22:10–24:00			

——— Required work hours
– – – Mandatory overtime, if required
········ Additional work time and time spent socializing with colleagues

*Manufacturing workers often work on Sunday based on production demands.
Source: Based on K. Bae, *Automobile Workers in Korea* (Seoul: Seoul National University Press, 1987), and personal interviews.

colleagues, thus yielding an average effective working time of something over ten hours per day.

This exceptional work ethic can be traced to the strong Confucian value system that pervades Korean society. This work ethic is found at all levels in the workplace and the educational system. It is known as *eui-yok*, which roughly translates as "will" or "ambition." A person who has *eui-yok* has an internal drive to succeed and has a mission to accomplish something important, more for the spiritual reward than for the financial reward. Several companies, most notably Sunkyong, consider *eui-yok* to be the "heart of the company." As noted by Sunkyong's Chairman Chey Jong-Hyon, the loss of *eui-yok* among employees leads to a loss of vitality that can easily destroy the capacity of the company to compete and survive (Son 1988; Office of the Chairman for Management and Planning, Sunkyong 1986). This internal drive—especially when it is expressed collectively instead of individually as in the West—explains why Koreans at all levels in the organization work hard on behalf of the company and why managers consider the preservation of this drive central to good management.

Achievement-oriented drive in Korea is unlike that found in the United States. Although ahievement-oriented individuals can be found in both countries, their behavior is focused quite differently. In Korea, the Confucian work ethic directs an employee's work effort to be primarily group oriented; the effort has a collective focus that emphasizes painstaking effort so the group (or company) will succeed. In the United States, by contrast, which embraces the Protestant work ethic, an employee's efforts are primarily individually oriented; it is important that the individual succeed and stand out in the group. Hence, while both countries experience a work ethic, its derivation and orientation are substantially different.

The argument also is made that Americans are rapidly losing their drive to work and succeed. As Daewoo's Chairman W. C. Kim (1983, 35) observed several years ago, "The American company is not what it used to be. In the old days, Americans worked hard to challenge new frontiers. But as their economy got mature, they became more interested in nice houses, jogging, and having a good time than in doing business. How can you compete without dedication? It is not the management system that is not working in American companies, it is the people not working hard." This difference between Korean and American work ethics and achievement orientations is illustrated in Exhibit 6–6, along with a similar comparison with Japan on various aspects of the work environment discussed below.

Group Harmony and the Social Contract

The second characteristic of a typical Korean work environment concerns what may be called the nature of the social contract. In Korea, the social contract is predicated on a firm belief in preserving group harmony. Lucky-Goldstar even has as its company motto *inhwa* (Korean for "harmony"), and ensuring harmony among employees is a theme repeated by executives from many companies. Like the work ethic, the principle of group harmony derives from Confucian thought, which stresses smooth, constructive, and conflict-free interpersonal relations at almost any cost.

Exhibit 6-6. Comparison of Work Environments in Korea, Japan, and the United States.

Characteristic	Korea	Japan	United States
Work ethic	High	High	Moderate to low
Focus of achievement	Group achievement	Group achievement	Individual achievement
Social contract	Preserve harmony	Preserve harmony	Ensure justice
Basis for career success	Seniority	Seniority and performance	Individual performance
Basis for superior-subordinate relationships	Paternalism	Paternalism	Bureaucratic model
Basis of business interactions	Personal relationships	Personal relationships	Legal contracts
Decisionmaking	Top down	Bottom up	Top down
Role of women	Subordinate	Subordinate	"Equal"

It can be argued that Korean (and Japanese) companies—and societies—emphasize preserving group harmony and that the West emphasizes preserving justice. That is, in the West, individuals or groups that think they have been unfairly treated will initiate a conflict (such as a lawsuit for sex discrimination) in order to resolve what they consider to be an injustice. This is common practice in the West and is seen by most people as fully acceptable behavior; the disharmony that results is an unfortunate side-effect of the pursuit of justice. In the East, by contrast, individuals often (although not always) are expected to subordinate their own plight or injustice in order to preserve the harmony of the larger group. For example, individual managers in many Asian (including Korean) companies may express support for equal employment rights for women, but they more than likely will also point out that to do so would create significant chaos in the managerial ranks and, as such, should be avoided. Preserving group harmony comes first.

In a sense, it is everyone's responsibility to maintain societal equilibrium, and this responsibility supersedes any conception of rights. In fact, in Korea and other Asian countries, one hears considerable talk about responsibilities to company and country and little about the individual's rights in either domain; in the West the ratio is typically just the opposite (see Exhibit 6-7). Westerners are often preoccupied with individual rights and seldom seriously consider individual responsibilities. In fact, when President John F. Kennedy said in his 1961 innaugural address, "Ask not what your country can do for you; ask what you can do for your country," it created quite a stir (and some action) in the Western world and is remembered almost thirty years later because of the uniqueness of the idea in American society. In Korea, such a statement by a new leader would never have received such attention; it would have been too commonplace an idea.

Basis for Career Success

A third variable in which differences can be noted between East and West is the central basis for career success. In most Western countries (including North America and Europe), career progression is based largely on the quality of an employee's job performance. Other

Exhibit 6-7. Relative Balance of Rights and Responsibilities: Korea versus United States.

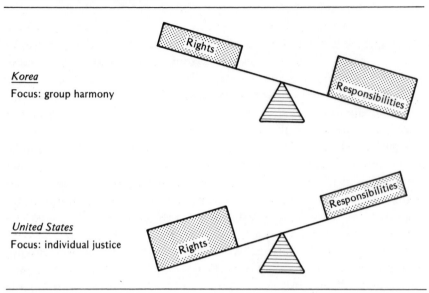

Korea
Focus: group harmony

United States
Focus: individual justice

factors enter into the promotion decision, but individual performance among managers emerges as a key variable.

By contrast, the central factor in determining career advancement in Korean firms is seniority. As is shown in Chapter 7, job performance is important (most companies use some form of performance evaluation) and other factors are considered, but seniority remains today the principal tool for advancement. This too follows from the Confucian tradition that strives to preserve harmony (since it is unseemly for younger employees to supervise older ones). It also is easier to use seniority to make promotion decisions than to rely on imprecise personnel evaluation methods to discriminate between a group of high achievers. Japan also gives considerable weight to seniority in such decisions, although it tends to rely more heavily than the Koreans on performance appraisals as an important input (see Exhibit 6-6). It should be noted, however, that as Korean firms move toward more professionalism in their management practices, greater emphasis is being placed on in-house performance evaluations for promotion decisions. Indeed, several companies (including Sunkyong) have used highly sophisticated performance evaluation systems for many years.

Paternalism in Superior-Subordinate Relationships

As might be expected from the above discussion, relationships between superiors and subordinates within an organization are characterized by a high degree of paternalism. A supervisor or manager is expected to assume personal responsibility for the development of his subordinates, and these subordinates are expected to respond by showing respect and obedience. There are mutual commitments and obligations. It is not uncommon for a manager to take his subordinates out drinking one night a week to discuss both business and personal matters and foster the harmonious atmosphere. Moreover, a manager is expected to take an active interest in his subordinate's personal and family life (attending funerals and birthday parties, gift-giving on certain occasions, and so forth). Like the Japanese, Korean companies share a "whole person" philosophy that stresses interrelationships among all parts of life. Conflict or problems at home may affect work performance and, as such, must be monitored and resolved.

This practice contrasts sharply with the typical Western norm that clearly separates worklife from homelife. In fact, U.S. employers are often legally proscribed from questioning employees about factors outside the workplace. In the United States superior-subordinate relationships tend to be more distant and less personal and are governed more by the rules of bureaucracy that prescribe detailed job responsibilities (after Weber 1947). The bureaucratic model began in Germany in the nineteenth century and spread to other Western nations as an ideal form of organization governed by rationality and merit, not favoritism or personal relationships. This model emphasizes clearly specified work rules that apply universally, employment and promotion based solely on merit and qualification, and the impersonality of office (that is, authority is invested in the office, not the individual, and office holders are expected to maintain an impersonal attitude when dealing with others). Under this system, paternalistic behavior is often resented as either being a form of favoritism or being too invasive of individual privacy. Individuals are responsible for taking care of themselves, and events outside of work are no one's business. In many Western companies, employees are actively discouraged from bringing their personal problems to work.

Job descriptions in the West also tend to be far longer and more specific in outlining required job duties than those in either Korea or Japan, where such descriptions simply define general parameters of the job. Seldom does an employee in Korea or Japan complain, "That's not my job!" In fact, the team atmosphere that pervades East Asian companies is greatly aided by these nonspecific job descriptions that encourage cooperative behavior for the good of the company.

Importance of Personal Relationships in Business

Because Koreans emphasize harmony and the West emphasizes justice, it is not surprising to discover that in business relationships Koreans give more credence to personal contacts and relationships while the West stresses written contracts. In Korea it is imperative that one be connected, both inside and outside the corporation. Considerable time is consumed in developing and nurturing personal relationships, and business deals (or simple favors) are predicated on such relationships. To most Korean businessmen, agreements between two parties change as business conditions change. Because mutual benefit of both parties is a goal, it would be inappropriate in many situations to hold one party to an agreement if business conditions change to his significant detriment. What is important is maintaining the personal relationship and enhancing mutual benefit, and a signed contract is simply a symbol of this.

Most managers in the West see business relationships very differently (Jang 1988; De Mente 1988). Contracts are the sine qui non of American business enterprise, and corporate lawyers and lawsuits proliferate in the United States. Personal relationships often are seen only as a means of securing a contract, and little effort (compared to Korea) is spent in nurturing them. This attitudinal difference becomes particularly important as more foreign businesses attempt to initiate trade or joint ventures in Korea.

Another aspect of this emphasis on personal relationships is the concept of *nunch'i*. *Nunch'i* translates roughly as "the look in someone's eyes." It is the nonverbal reaction of someone to a question, an order, or a comment, and Korean businessmen pride themselves on their ability to read someone's face. In developing personal relationships and in other forms of social interaction, nonverbal behavior is far more important in the East than the West, and success in these interactions depends on one's ability to read *nunch'i*—that is, the ability to silently understand what the other party is thinking. In fact, there is a Korean proverb that translates "One who does not have *nunch'i* cannot succeed." Moreover, in interpersonal interactions, most Koreans typically assume that the other party also has this capability. Thus, if an employee asked for a favor that his supervisor either could not or would not grant, the supervisor could use *nunch'i* to signal his negative response, thereby avoiding a loss of face to either party by formally (and publicly) declining the request. In contrast to the West, what Koreans do not say is often far more important than they do say, and one's ability to interpret this silent language accurately is essential for career or business success.

Decisionmaking in Organizations

Significant variations can be found in the decisionmaking processes used in various Korean companies. Most international observers are familiar with the Japanese *ringi-sei* decisionmaking system, whereby proposals work their way up from the bottom of the organization so that by the time the proposal reaches top management there is widespread consensus as to the desired course of action. In theory, Korean business organizations use the same system. In Korean, it is called *pummi*, or "proposal submitted for deliberation" (*pummi* and *ringi-sei* use the same Chinese characters). In Korea, however, the *pummi* approach is seldom followed in any systematic fashion in the big companies, with the possible exception of Daewoo, where consensus-building takes on critical importance. Instead, the *pummi* system tends to serve other purposes; namely, to provide documentation for all company programs and new ventures and to diffuse responsibility for decision implementation.

In more cases than many managers care to admit, decisionmaking in Korean companies is typically highly centralized in the hands of top executives who make decisions either unilaterally or in small groups after consultation with the various parties involved. Several years ago, Vroom and Yetton (1973) identified a continuum of three general types of decisionmaking: authoritarian, where the executive makes the decision himself based on information sometimes provided by others; consultative, where the executive first consults with interested subordinates to learn their views and then makes a solitary decision; and group, where the executive attempts to the extent possible to allow the affected group to make the decision.

Using this model, the Japanese *ringi-sei* system comes closest to the group decisionmaking method, although exceptions can be found. Evidence suggests that most Korean companies tend to fall somewhere between the authoritarian and the participative approaches and are more top-down oriented than comparable Japanese companies. Companies that are owner-managed tend to be somewhat more authoritarian, and those that rely heavily on professional managers tend to be somewhat more participative. In either case, however, more participative methods generally are used in the managerial hierarchy and more authoritarian methods are used in the blue-collar ranks. It should also be noted here that even under the so-called authoritarian approach to management, Confucian tradition requires the decisionmaker to balance the needs and harmony of the group with business demands, a phenomenon Western managers often fail to understand.

A diversity in decisionmaking styles is also found in the United States, where some companies (such as Hewlett-Packard and IBM) are known for their highly participative styles, while others exhibit more authoritarian styles. In either case, however, American (and Korean) companies seldom approach the Japanese in terms of fostering genuine bottom-up consensus building around a proposed course of action.

One final difference concerning decision implementation is noted here. In the United States a fundamental principle of good management is that authority must be delegated down to the level where responsibility to carry out the decision lies. In other words, the person assigned responsibility to accomplish a certain task must be given sufficient authority on matters that directly affect task accomplishment. In East Asia, by contrast, it is not uncommon to observe situations where authority is centralized but responsibility is decentralized. A junior manager, for example, may be told in essence, "You didn't choose this course of action, but you must make it work." Once an executive decision is made to enter a new and risky business or take over an old failing one, despite widespread belief that the decision was in error, subordinates do not question the action; their job is to make the venture successful against all odds. In contrast to the typical situation in the West, such individuals are held personally responsible for project success and not just for giving it their best effort.

Role of Women in Organizations

A key factor in the economic success of many Korean firms is the large pool of young, highly skilled and motivated—but poorly paid—female workers. Only 26 percent of the women over fourteen years of age are employed (compared to 36 percent in Japan and over 40 percent in the United States), but the limited range of opportunities results in an ample pool of well-qualified applicants (Shrader 1986). Most working women are young and unmarried and work either as assemblers on a production line or clerical workers in an office. The average age for employed women is twenty-four, compared to thirty-one for men, and most companies require women to resign on marriage or retire at thirty, even if single.

An average work day in an office typically runs from 8:30 A.M. to 6:30 or 7:30 P.M. In exchange for this, women tend to receive about 80 percent of the salaries of their male counterparts working on similar jobs. Annual salary increases are minimal, and promotions to important positions within the company are extremely rare. College graduates fare somewhat better and receive about 15 percent more salary than their high school counterparts; they also have somewhat higher status within the organization (see Exhibit 6–2 earlier in the chapter). Although a small number of women are finding their way into white-collar positions, primarily in the areas of personnel or translation services, Korean tradition prefers that they remain at home (*Business Korea* 1986). Women are clearly viewed as temporary workers and are typically treated as such in most companies.

KOREAN MANAGEMENT IN THE UNITED STATES

Like the Japanese, several Korean companies have begun to operate manufacturing facilities in the United States. This move may have been largely prompted by a desire to be closer to their major markets and to defuse protectionist sentiments in Congress. To date, two major facilities have begun operations, although many smaller ones are also present. First to begin actual operation (in 1982) was Goldstar of America, in Huntsville, Alabama, followed by Samsung International in New Jersey in 1984. As noted in Chapter 4, both facilities manufacture electronic equipment, such as televisions, VCRs, and microwave ovens, and both have attempted to transfer modified Korean management techniques to the new operations.

At the Goldstar facility, all senior managers except the personnel manager are Korean. This practice of having a local personnel person surrounded by "foreign" management is also typical of U.S. plants operated by the Japanese. But as Goldstar President, P. W. Suh explains, all workers are considered part of the "family": "We emphasize teamwork. I have tried to make a mixture between the good points of Korean management and the good points of the American way" (1986, 35). This includes efforts to maintain open communications and an emphasis on quality control. As Suh notes, "Step by step they [the American workers] are understanding the company's mind. If the company grows, then they will too" (1986, 35).

Employees at the Goldstar plant are primarily female (72 percent) and follow a normal American work schedule of five eight-hour days per week (Shorrock 1986). The Korean managers at the plant, however, usually maintain a Korean work schedule of seventy to eighty hours per week, compared to sixty to seventy hours for Japanese managers in the United States and forty-five hours for American managers (Baum 1987). The company (and community) is staunchly anti-union, as apparently are the employees. The incentive program for employees combines an emphasis on a positive work environment (especially open communications) with a bonus system to supplement the relatively low wages.

To facilitate a family work environment, supervisors meet for thirty minutes every Monday morning to discuss product requirements for the week. At monthly meetings, plant managers meet with employees to discuss productivity, give awards for excellence, and listen to feedback from employees concerning problems at work. Once a quarter, President Suh meets with employees, and he maintains an open-door policy for employees who wish to talk personally. The company also sponsors one major activity each month, such as a picnic or volleyball tournament. Through such techniques, the company hopes to create the *inhwa* atmosphere that Korean businesses thrive on.

In addition, a "production incentive plan" provides one hour of overtime pay if workers meet their daily production quota "with quality products." If the quota is exceeded, they receive another hour's pay, and employees receive $50 each month for perfect attendance (including both being at work every day and not being tardy). Attendance at Goldstar is around 1 percent, compared to the national norm of 7 percent.

The work environment at Samsung is similar, as are the positive results (Baum 1987). The Samsung approach to corporate culture is also opposed to a unionized workforce. Indeed, a 1985 union organizing election at Samsung in the labor state of New Jersey was defeated by a nine-to-one margin. In commenting on the operations of Goldstar and Samsung, long-time Korea observer Karl Moskowitz (1987: 1) concludes: "The success of Korean companies in motivating and managing American blue-collar workers is the result of the flip-side of this authoritarianism [endemic in the Korean managerial style]: an extreme paternalism that emphasizes direct emotional ties and responsibility for employees (not from the group, as in Japan, but from above), as well as the distinctly Korean cultural emphasis on openly emotional personal ties." Korean managers seem obsessed with "taking care of their people."

Meanwhile, Korean executives in Seoul talk openly about their American successes and about their plans for U.S. expansion. They readily admit, too, that a key to this success is the effort made by the companies to blend what they believe to be the positive aspects of Korean management style with American realities to achieve a workable balance that benefits all parties. And the Koreans claim they are in the United States to stay.

7 PERSONNEL POLICIES AND LABOR RELATIONS

By any standard of comparison, the sprawling Samsung electronics facility at Suwon is impressive. It is one of the largest and most technologically advanced integrated research and manufacturing facilities in the world and is the pride of the company. It symbolizes Samsung's commitment to being a major world-class player in the field of consumer electronics. It also can provide considerable insight into the managerial and personnel practices that have contributed to the success of Korean corporations.

Within this massive complex can be found assembly-line workers like Hwang Jo Yon and Hur Jang Mee. Like most workers on the line, Hwang and Hur are both young unmarried women with high school degrees and probably will remain with the company for four or five years until they marry. Hwang and Hur both applied to Samsung because of the company's reputation for being a good employer. They were among the one-third of all applicants accepted by the company for such positions (Magaziner and Patinkin 1989).

On arrival at the complex both young women were given blue uniforms and two weeks of training and were assigned to the microwave oven assembly line. On the line, they work eleven hours a day, twenty-seven days a month, the same schedule that is worked by even the most senior people. This averages out to about sixty-eight hours per week. In exchange for this, they earn a base wage (in 1988) of just over $350 per month, or about $1.20 per hour. In addition, medical services and lunches are free, and breakfasts and dinners can be purchased for 15 cents. They receive ten days off for vacation, five in the summer and five in the winter. If they wish, they can spend this time at company-run resorts. During various times throughout the year, the workers also receive gifts, such as clothes, shoes, hiking bags, and tape recorders (made by Samsung, of course). Housing is provided free in company-sponsored dormitories. Each of the fifteen dormitories for women houses 420 people, six to a room.

The women get up at 6:00 A.M. and have breakfast by 7:00; they then go to the factory. Once at work in the microwave oven assembly facility, Hwang's job is to attach 1,200 oven doors per day, while Hur attaches 1,200 labels. Both claim that quality is very important to them and that they do their best to produce a perfect product every time. After work, they must be back in the dormitories by 9:30 P.M., even on the three Sundays off they receive each month. The next morning, they get up and go to work.

In many ways, the story of Hwang and Hur is typical of assembly-line work in Korea. Such stories illustrate the dedication and commitment to hard work that characterizes most employees. They also provide us with a glimpse of how Korean firms manage their human resources, for without these stringent yet apparently widely accepted personnel practices, the Korean miracle could not have happened. The general characteristics of Korean personnel practices and the state of labor relations are the focus of this chapter. Differences clearly exist across companies, but a portrait of the typical or average company can examine such variables as recruitment and selection, training and development, compensation and benefits, performance evaluation and promotion, and retirement as well as the current state of labor-management relations. The information presented in this chapter was gathered both from archival data and extensive interviews with executives at various companies.

In tracing the development of human resource management in Korean firms, Professor Shin Yoo Keun (1988a) of Seoul National University has pointed out that such practices resulted from largely two forces. The original—and currently the strongest—force emerges from the Confucian tradition that permeates much of Korean society. In this tradition originates corporate concern for values such as hard work, dedication, seniority, and absolute loyalty to the company. The second force shaping human resource management in Korea is the contemporary push to implement "modern" (typically Western) approaches to management and personnel development. Companies are concerned with making improvements in practices such as employee recruitment, employee training, performance appraisals, and so forth. Shin argues that the increasing tendency toward these newer approaches has been facilitated by executive decisions to make personnel policies more "scientific." These decisions, in turn, have been encouraged by changes in the economic, social, technological, and political environments surrounding the corporations. For these reasons, corporations have begun moving away from the traditional approach toward a more professional approach to management.

RECRUITMENT AND SELECTION

Corporate recruiting methods vary considerably according to factors like company size and the positions being filled. At the blue-collar level, it has been estimated that a large number of all jobs are filled through what has been termed "back door recruitment" (DeMente 1988). This involves hiring someone either because he is recommended by a friend or relative who is already employed by the firm or at the very least hiring someone who heard about the job through such channels. It is often felt that such techniques lead to good employees, since the company already has someone on the payroll who will vouch for the sincerity and dedication of the candidate.

In addition, many jobs are filled through "open recruitment," where prospective job candidates hear about openings through public announcements or through direct inquiries. About 10 percent of blue-collar hires come from vocational school placements. Graduates of technical high schools and vocational training institutes must obtain a skill-test certificate from the National Skill Testing Agency, while graduates of other high schools usually must pass company entrance examinations or have the support of a strong connection within the company. Some of the largest corporations, such as Hyundai and Samsung, manage their own vocational training institutes to ensure a steady supply of well-trained workers.

As might be expected, smaller companies tend to rely less on open recruitment and testing and more on personal connections in recruiting blue-collar employees. This is also true of companies located in rural areas of Korea (Shin 1988a).

At the white-collar level, applicants are often actively recruited from the better-known universities. Most applicants must pass company-sponsored entrance examinations that typically include English language proficiency in addition to knowledge in both a major field and general abilities or common sense. Moreover, applicants must pass through extensive interviews (sometimes with the chairman of the company) and reference checks. New college graduates are preferred to people with experience, and once hired, the new employees are typically assigned to such core departments as planning, finance, and accounting after a relatively short training period. This contrasts with U.S. practices, which value previous work experience and which typically assign new employees to a functional department based on their specialty. It also contrasts somewhat with Japanese companies in that new employees in Japan are more likely to begin with a job in the field.

Managerial Selection at Sunkyong

Consider the application and screening process for salarymen at the Sunkyong Group. Sunkyong is a diversified corporation that now ranks as the fifth-largest concern on Korea. With about $8 billion in sales, the company has its base in petrochemicals, energy, and textiles, although it is also involved in general trading, transportation, construction, and hotels. Under the leadership of Chairman Choy Jong Hyon, corporate strategy relies on vertical integration. In fact, Yukong, Ltd., a group company that is emerging as the forerunner of the integrated energy business sector, accounted for 46 percent of the total group's turnover and 57 percent of its net income for 1988 (C. S. Bae 1988). The company attributes its success to a combination of high technology and human resources.

Sunkyong has been an industry leader in the development of highly sophisticated personnel policies that are designed to secure the best possible employees. Referred to as the Sunkyong Management System (or SKMS), Sunkyong has taken a systematic approach to management that incorporates the traditional management functions with a dynamic concern for developing employees to their fullest. Central to this model is the notion of *eui-yok management*, which is defined as providing the conditions under which individuals and groups can draw satisfaction from and take pride in their work

(Office of the Chairman for Management and Planning, Sunkyong Group 1986).

Because it is often identified in surveys as one of Korea's most preferred employers (C. S. Bae 1988), Sunkyong can afford to be highly selective in its new hires. In its policy manuals, the company identifies six primary criteria for selection: (1) *pae-gie*, meaning "the spirit to get the job done and win the business," (2) business knowledge, (3) business-related knowledge, such as foreign language expertise or practical science knowledge, (4) social attitudes and interpersonal skills, (5) home management, including having a stable home life, and (6) health management, including physical and mental wellbeing (Sunkyong Group, 1986, 1987). Within the company, these six criteria are referred to as the principles of "SK-manship."

When selecting new employees, information concerning these six criteria are collected from screening documents, aptitude tests, personality tests, interviews, and physical examinations. Letters of recommendation are requested from outsiders, and reviewers are asked

Exhibit 7-1. Criteria and Information Sources for Managerial Selection at Sunkyong.

SK-manship	Document Screening	Aptitude Test	Personality Test	Interview	Physical Exam
Pae-gie*			●	●	
Business knowledge	●	●		●	
Business-related knowledge	●	●		●	
Social attitude			●	●	
Home management			●	●	
Health management				●	●

Pae-gie translates roughly as "the spirit to get the job done and win the business" and is similar in meaning to need for achievement.

Source: Translated and adapted from Sunkyong Corporation, Office of the Chairman for Management and Planning, "Outline of Human Resources Management" (Seoul, 1987).

to rate the candidate's "positive thinking," "progressive action," "responsibility," and "social attitude." Finally, applicants are asked to complete an extensive self-report inventory that includes demographic data plus a self-appraisal on variables such as leadership, sociability, ambition, responsibility, and self-control. Professional personnel staff then review all this information and assign points to decide who to hire.

A summary of the factors going into this process is shown in Exhibit 7–1. Throughout the process, the aim is to secure a small number of highly skilled and highly motivated employees who can fit into the company's culture and make a long-term commitment to develop and grow with the company.

TRAINING AND DEVELOPMENT

Korean companies, like their Japanese counterparts, view human resources as the central building block for corporate success and invest considerable effort in the development of employees at all levels. At the blue-collar level, the primary instructional methods involve on-the-job training aimed at improving job-related skills and correct attitudes toward the company. As these employees gain experience, the focus of training shifts to the development of future first-line supervisors for the company. At this level, the approach to training is not unlike that found in many industrialized countries of the world, including the United States.

At the managerial level, however, the objectives and methods of corporate training and development are somewhat different than those found in the West. The focus is less on gaining new job-related knowledge or skills and more on molding managers and future managers to fit into the company's corporate culture. Emphasis is placed on developing positive attitudes over professional skills under the assumption that loyalty, dedication, and team spirit are more important than current job skills. As the companies see it, their aim is to develop what is often called the "all-around man." The all-around man possesses general abilities; he is not a specialist. His commitment to the company and his coworkers is unquestioned, and above all he fits into the group. Training is seen as one means to ensure this across the corporation. Two examples from Daewoo and Hyundai should serve to illustrate this point.

Management Training at Daewoo

At Daewoo, the Education and Training Department reports directly to the Office of Planning and Coordination (see Chapter 3). The executive director for education and training oversees and is responsible for all corporate developmental efforts. Many years ago, the company established a clear link between the development of employees and the development of the company, as can be seen in a 1984 statement of the basic principles for corporate training (see Exhibit 7-2). In this statement, Daewoo expressed the belief that its business philosophy and its business spirit (creativity, challenge, and self-sacrifice) are both directly influenced by the cultivation of Daewoo peronnel. This, in turn, is influenced by the company's training

Exhibit 7-2. Basic Principles for Corporate Training at Daewoo.

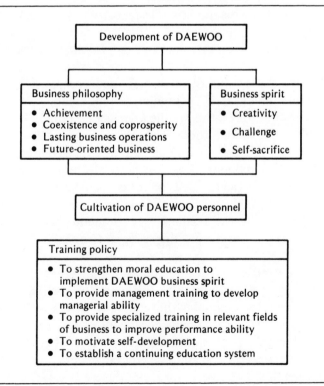

Source: Adapted from Daewoo Corporation, Education and Training Department, Planning and Coordination Division, "Education and Training at Daewoo," Seoul, 1984.

policies (Daewoo Corporation 1984, 6). Six principal training objectives were identified:

1. To implement the Daewoo business philosophy and business spirit;
2. To develop managerial techniques and improve professional knowledge and specialized ability;
3. To foster adaptability to meet changing business environments;
4. To maximize organizational efficiency;
5. To enhance the special identity of Daewoo employees;
6. To motivate self-development.

A number of specific training programs are offered to facilitate these objectives. We mention four here as illustrative of the variety and depth of such programs. At the entry level for new employees destined for managerial positions, Daewoo offers the Newcomers' Training Program. This program lasts eleven days and nights and includes the following topics: (1) "Daewoo-manship" and the business philosophy, (2) an introduction to affiliated companies of the Daewoo Group, (3) a case study of job performance, (4) freshman's life planning, (5) a tour through affiliated companies, (6) a team demonstration, and (7) a VCR tape of the chairman.

Moving up the ladder, the Middle Manager's Training Program consists of fifteen days and focuses on improving managerial abilities, especially those relating to human resource management. Emphasis is also placed on understanding corporate strategy. Once a manager reaches the director level, he is sent to the Advanced Management Training Program. This consists of four days and examines such topics as understanding the business environment and long-range corporate strategy. In addition, this program includes talks with the chairman.

Finally, in a move that is uncommon for a Korean company, Daewoo offers training programs for the wives of their managers. For directors' wives, for example, the company offers a three-day program that includes the following topics: (1) Daewoo's business philosophy and spirit, (2) the relationship between office and home, (3) educational lectures, (4) "economic common sense," and (5) "what's a happy home life?" The basic thrust of the wives' program is to demonstrate that the entire household—not just the husband—belongs to the Daewoo family and that the husband's success is influenced by a supportive homelife.

Thus, regardless of the level, Daewoo is committed to developing its managerial personnel through a series of fairly sophisticated programs tailored to the short- and long-range goals of the company.

Management Training at Hyundai

The Hyundai Management Development Institute (HMDI) is located in a modern campus-like setting in the beautiful countryside near Yonginkun in Kyunggi-do. HMDI represents a sizable investment for Hyundai: The facility contains modern classrooms, extensive language and computer laboratories, and a variety of physical fitness facilities, including an Olympic-sized swimming pool, and has dormitory space for close to 500 managers.

In July 1988 HMDI was under the direction of M. C. Shin, who reported directly to the honorary chairman of the Hyundai Group. Chairman Chung, the founder of Hyundai, strongly believed in the importance of developing human potential, and corporate training was seen as a primary means to this end. He established two committees to oversee the Institute's operation: the Group Committee on Training, which focuses on developing plans and strategies for managerial training from the corporate perspective, and the Implementing Committee, which consists of one member from each of the group companies and is charged with implementing the general strategies set forth by the first committee.

A three-part general philosophy underlies the training efforts at the Institute: the importance of (1) working for the further development of Korea, (2) developing human resources, and (3) forging international relationships and a global orientation. In support of this philosophy, three training objectives have been set forth: (1) to incorporate the Hyundai spirit in the manager's daily life, (2) to develop managerial skills and capabilities, and (3) to strengthen international competitiveness. Finally, on an operational level, three implementing principles guide actual program design and implementation. Thus, each program includes components relating to the development of (1) managerial and technical skills, (2) mental skills, including a heavy emphasis on what are termed "oriental values" such as creativity, positive thinking, tenacity, fraternity, devotion to company, and industriousness, and (3) physical capabilities, including mandatory physical exercise beginning at 6:30 A.M. each morning. These three implementing principles aim to develop what the company refers to as the "Hyundai man."

HMDI offers five kinds of programs. These programs include top management executive training, midlevel managers programs, professional courses (such as accounting or job skills), language training, and courses to train trainers. Courses for top and middle managers cover different topics each year, and a typical course lasts three to four days. Teaching methods are diverse and include lectures, case analyses, experiential exercises, and in-basket techniques. Instructors come both from the company staff and from prestigious university business schools. According to Shin, the Institute's biggest problem is scheduling the many diverse programs because demand for course offerings is significant. Hyundai has as a matter of policy established the goal of having each of the 13,000 managers in the company visit the training institute a minimum of once every other year, even if only for a few days. Clearly training is important for this company.

COMPENSATION AND BENEFITS

Employee compensation is always difficult to examine. Information is often confidential, incomplete, or misleading. Moreover, given the volatile labor situation in Korea today, any specific data currently available could be subject to rather dramatic changes. Within these limitations this section provides a general description of the compensation and benefit policies of the major Korean firms.

It must be recognized that even with the recent sizable pay raises given to workers, the average Korean employee—both blue-collar and white-collar—works longer hours than his or her counterparts in other countries (including newly industrialized countries or NICs) and often receives less money for doing so. One study by T. W. Kang (1989) using 1987 data illustrates this point. As shown in Exhibit 7-3, average Korean wage levels ($4,224 per year) are significantly below Singapore ($5,087) and Taiwan ($5,290), although they are above wages in Hong Kong and Malaysia. Such wages do not even begin to compare with those in Japan ($22,458). Moreover, as

Exhibit 7–3. 1987 Wage Levels for Selected Countries.

Country	Wage Level
Japan	$22,458
Taiwan	5,290
Singapore	5,087
Korea	4,224
Hong Kong	3,460
Malaysia	1,560

Source: Adapted from T. W. Kang, *Is Korea the Next Japan?* (New York: Free Press, 1989).

noted in Chapter 6, the average hours worked per year in Korea are significantly longer than those worked in Japan, the United States, or Western Europe.

Wages in Korea are comprised of three factors: basic wages, allowances, and bonuses. The *basic wage* is the largest and most important part of the wage package and consists of the employee's starting wage plus annual increments and cost-of-living adjustments. Starting salaries are determined largely by educational level and initial point of entry into the company. This, in turn, is influenced at least to some extent by external market rates (university graduates with science or technical backgrounds, for example, generally receive a higher starting salary that those with business degrees). Currently, high school graduates begin at salaries that are approximately 85 percent of those received by college graduates, compared to 70 percent in the United States and 80 percent in Japan.

Annual salary increases are determined largely by seniority or tenure and, to a much lesser degree, merit. The concept of "pay for performance" or merit compensation is largely avoided because a seniority system is felt to contribute more toward the maintenance of group harmony. Thus, over time, employee salaries tend to progress slowly upward for everyone as a group. The one exception to this occurs among production workers, who often see real pay decreases after the age of fifty due presumably to their reduced physical contribution to the company.

The second component of the wage package consists of a set of *allowances* granted to employees. Allowances can take several forms. For example, the Korean Labor Standards Act requires employers to pay overtime equal to one-and-one-half times regular pay for each additional hour worked beyond eight hours (S. K. Kim 1987). For white-collar employees, an overtime allowance of two hours per day is typically automatically added to one's pay. One-and-one-half times the base wage is also paid to employees working from 10:00 P.M. to 6:00 A.M. Employers are also required to provide workers with eight days' paid leave for one full year's service without absence; each absence is subtracted from this total. Employees also typically receive one day of paid vacation per year for each year of tenure (that is, five days annual paid vacation after five years of service), and after twenty vacation days are accumulated employees can take the extra days in wages instead of time off. In most Korean companies, like their Japanese counterparts, few employees actually take all the vacation time to which they are entitled, to avoid showing disloyalty toward the company.

Female employees are entitled to one day's paid leave per month and sixty days' paid leave for pregnancy. Beyond what is required by law for both males and females, many companies offer additional allowances for such things as being assigned to a remote area, having an official skills certificate, possessing skills that are in short supply, and having a large number of dependents. Housing and car allowances are also common. In case of death, it is customary for the company to provide 1,000 days of wages plus funeral expenses to the family. All told, allowances often constitute about 30 percent of the employee's pay package.

The complexity of factors that comprise the Korean pay system has led many companies to employ a unique approach to calculating actual compensation—the "reverse calculation system" (RCS). Under RCS, the employer pays employees a fixed monthly amount that is based on a formula estimate of all the expenses associated with the employee's allowances. This simplifies having to calculate each benefit for each employee on a monthly basis, and the Korean government has generally held that such an approach is within the statutes of the Korean Labor Standards Act.

Finally, the third part of the wage package consists of employee *bonuses.* Although ostensibly based on company performance and not required by law, bonuses have come to be an expected part of the compensation system, in part because of the relatively low salaries paid to employees. The typical large company pays annual bonuses amounting to about four to six months' gross salary (referred to as a "400 percent" or a "600 percent" bonus); smaller companies typically pay somewhat less than this. Bonuses are usually paid out four times per year (to coincide with New Year's Day, the beginning of summer vacation, Korean Thanksgiving Day, and Christmas). The majority of companies provide bonuses in equal amounts according to one's level in the hierarchy. Even those companies that give differential bonuses (that is, giving different bonus amounts to employees at the same level) typically give 90 percent of the employees on each level the same amount. Most managers believe that in view of the cooperative nature of work it is simply not possible to differentiate performance levels between employees with any degree of accuracy. It also disturbs the harmony. The amount of the bonus can vary depending on business conditions, but some companies continue to pay the bonus even during difficult economic times in order to show goodwill and maintain harmony within their workforce.

PERFORMANCE EVALUATION AND PROMOTION

All large and most small Korean companies use some form of an annual performance appraisal system. The primary emphasis in evaluations at the blue-collar and lower managerial levels is on employee development, since promotion is largely based on seniority. (For salarymen, the first promotion usually comes after three to four years.) Companies take these evaluations very seriously because they represent a part of the human resource management process, and managers feel a special responsibility to help develop employees below them since these are the future leaders of the company. As mentioned earlier, in this process evaluators look carefully at the "whole man," and factors such as sincerity, loyalty, proper attitude, and initiative are at least as important as actual job performance.

At the higher levels of management, more emphasis is placed on actual performance and contribution to the company (instead of seniority) as a determining factor in promotions. In some companies—particularly those involved in high technology—"star players," who move on a fast track toward the top, emerge. Even so, seniority still plays an important role in determining who gets ahead at these higher echelons.

Performance Appraisal at Sunkyong

One of the most comprehensive performance appraisal systems in Korea can be found at Sunkyong. Like other companies, Sunkyong's approach emphasizes employee development. The goals set forth for the evaluation process include identifying employee inadequacies or weaknesses in need of correction, developing managerial capabilities, and enhancing the company's human resource management process. Sunkyong's system begins with an extensive self-assessment inventory tory by the employee. Employees are asked to complete this inventory accurately and sincerely, evaluating themselves on factors such as "SK-manship," managerial capacity, communication, coordination, and their adequacy for and satisfaction with their present assignment, as well as identifying anything that may be obstructing their improvement on each factor. Employees are also asked to describe how their job performance has contributed to company well-being and how they feel about general company administration.

This inventory then becomes input for interviews (and written reports) first by the employee's immediate supervisor and later by the supervisor's supervisor. Peer assessments from co-workers are also sought. Through extensive discussions, efforts are made to reach agreement concerning the employee's strengths and weaknesses and a plan of action for self-improvement. Ultimately, the written material goes to the corporate HRM department for final disposition and approval. Throughout, emphasis is placed on developing the employee's long-term potential as a Sunkyong manager. In order to accomplish this, considerable effort is devoted to developing a trusting relationship between superiors and subordinates and ensuring shared mutual expectations for the future of the company.

Keys to Managerial Success

In interviews with various corporate executives, we sought information concerning the "ideal" manager. What, in other words, are the keys to managerial success, and how do companies identify these characteristics when hiring new employees? Interviews in companies like Lucky-Goldstar, Samsung, Daewoo, Doosan, Sunkyong, Kumho, and others yielded similar results. The ideal young candidate for most companies was both smart and highly motivated. He exhibited a strong work ethic and a positive attitude toward hard work for company and country. Personal initiative was important. He had a good character and background and was willing to learn. Finally, he presented himself well and was comfortable to be around. Some companies also indicated that the ideal candidate was a risk-taker who had the capacity to make rapid and incisive decisions under pressure.

At Samsung, for example, which hires between 3,000 and 4,000 people per year and has a selection ratio of about 4 to 1, native intelligence was the first characteristic considered. Initial screening for this was made based on written tests. Tests were followed by a series of interviews in which company officials examined interpersonal factors such as initiative, personal responsibility, and interpersonal style. At times, two candidates would be put into a debate with each other to see how they performed under pressure. Throughout the process, the company tried to select those candidates with the greatest potential to develop into long-term, committed, and useful employees for Samsung.

TERMINATIONS, LAYOFFS, AND RETIREMENT

Termination of employees is legal in Korea as long as the company can show just cause (under the Korean Labor Standards Act). Under such circumstances, the employer must provide either thirty days' notice or one month's salary. In addition, severance pay equivalent to one month's salary for each year of continuous service must be paid.

Layoffs are not uncommon in Korea, and the concept of "lifetime" employment is rarely seen, in contrast to Japan. Instead, companies typically rely on a strategy of continued corporate growth and expansion to ensure fairly stable employment. When layoffs are necessary, companies often encourage older workers or female employees of marriageable age to leave and provide extra financial incentives to do so. Given Korea's extended family system, in which the incomes of all family members are often pooled, such laid-off employees are absorbed back into the family and provided for.

Retirement is mandatory in most cases at age fifty-five. Retiring employees typically receive a lump-sum payment equal to one month's salary for each year of service. Few employees are offered part-time work or consulting work with the company after retirement, as is seen in Japan.

LABOR RELATIONS

Labor relations and the collective bargaining process in Korea are in a state of flux. As recently as the early 1980s, only minimal labor disputes occurred because employees at all levels felt that sacrifice was essential if the company and the country were to succeed. The country's labor laws, especially the 1980 revision of the Korean Labor Standards Act, encouraged the establishment of enterprise (or company) unions, instead of industrial or trade unions. This practice limited a union's ability to organize and bargain collectively. Strikes were severely limited. It was even illegal for an enterprise union to accept advice or assistance from the national Federation of Korean Trade Unions. Some observers felt that the governments position was that strong labor unions were "conflictful, unproductive, and disruptive in the context of economic growth" (Choi 1983, 282). Union membership remained relatively low at 1.5 million people, or about one-tenth of the eligible workforce (*Economist* 1988b).

Korean labor laws (especially the Labor-Management Council Act as revised in 1988) mandated that every company with over fifty employees create a works council, or *nosa hyeobeuihoe*, designed much along the lines of those found in Western Europe. These councils were seen as a substitute for labor unions in handling labor-management relations. In theory, these works councils provided for equal labor and management representation and served as a means of democratizing the workplace and providing for labor-management cooperation and productivity enhancement. In practice, however, management typically controlled the works councils, which lost their potential as an agent for real change in the workplace.

The works council at Hyundai Motor Company (Bae 1987) during most of the 1980s consisted of twelve management representatives (including the factory's chief executive officer, the personnel director, and ten members selected by the CEO) and twelve members elected annually by the workers. The council was required to meet at least once every three months but could meet more often if it so chose. Agenda items that could be discussed at the council were clearly specified: (1) how to improve productivity and efficiency at work, (2) how to educate and train workers, (3) how to prevent labor-management disputes, (4) how to handle workers' grievances, (5) how to promote workers' interests, (6) how to increase safety and improve the work environment, and (7) how to increase labor-management cooperation. Other issues were not allowed. Regulations governing the council also stipulated that (1) the purpose of the council was to foster labor-management cooperation and industrial peace, (2) members of the council should not engage in any behavior that might encourage a labor-management dispute or break the industrial peace, and (3) the council could not be used for collective bargaining.

Many workers, however, felt that these regulations put them in an impossible situation. The law governing works councils required that all worker demands had to be channeled through the works councils, yet real collective bargaining was proscribed. All workers at Hyundai could do was express their grievances to management; they had no mechanism to require management to consider their demands.

This system continued to function throughout most of the 1980s but changed dramatically in 1987. As Korean companies and the country as a whole became increasingly more prosperous, workers and unions began a concerted drive to improve both wages and working conditions. The number of strikes rose from around 100 per year to over 3,800 in 1987 and continued into 1988 and 1989. Underlying these strikes was a widespread feeling by workers that the Korean economic miracle was not being shared equally throughout the country. In fact, it was felt that the miracle itself had occurred only as a result of the sacrifice of the Korean workforce and that the time had come for a return on that investment. Evidence for such feelings can be seen in Exhibit 7-4, which indicates that real wages in Korea had fallen substantially behind the nation's gross domestic product (GDP). Real wages also lagged far behind industrywide productivity gains. When President Roh took power in 1988, his administration carefully avoided interfering in the labor turmoil other than to call for calm and renewed efforts at labor-management cooperation. An era of collective bargaining had begun.

The strikes were hard fought and cost the Korean economy dearly, but they led to major pay increases across broad segments of the

Exhibit 7-4.   Increases in Korean Gross Domestic Product and Real Wages, 1978–87.

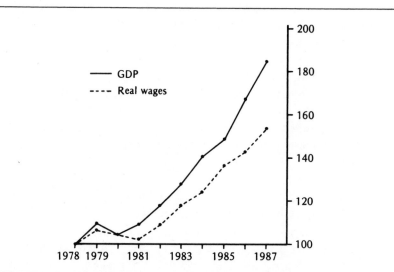

Source: Based on data reported in "South Korea: Contentment Has Its Price," *The Economist*, 23 July 1988, p. 34. Note: 1978 equals 100.

workforce. In 1987 the average pay increase in the industrial sector was 22 percent. This was followed in 1988 by an additional 15 percent average pay raise. Hence, in two years, wage rates—and labor costs—rose 37 percent (see Exhibit 7–5). Korea was no longer a cheap labor country, and Korean companies began almost at once to look for cheaper sites offshore (most notably China, Indonesia, Malaysia, and Thailand) for their production and manufacturing needs.

To see how these changes affected a typical working man, consider the example of Park Jin Woo, an assembly-line worker at Daewoo Motor Company (*Asia Week* 1988). Park is twenty-seven and participated in a forty-day strike at Daewoo to secure higher wages. He received a 30 percent pay raise and now earns $350 per month. Even so, a fifth of his salary goes for rent on a one-room apartment he shares with six other family members, and he still worries if he will have to borrow money if one of his children becomes ill. "We have a long way to go," says Park as he considers the events of the past two years. So apparently does Daewoo. The strike cost the company over $200 million, which led the company to raise prices on its

Exhibit 7-5. Average Salary Increases for Korean Factory Workers, 1985-88.

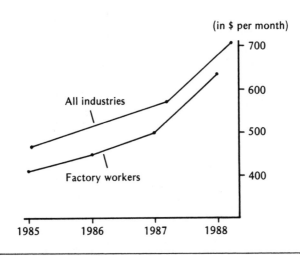

Source: Korean Economic Planning Board as reported in "Bigger Raises for Korean Workers," *Business Week*, 10 April 1989, p. 45. Reprinted by special permission, copyright © 1989 by McGraw-Hill, Inc.

exported cars, thereby making them less competitive in the international marketplace. Daewoo is looking seriously at increasing factory automation and decreasing the number of workers it requires. From the company's standpoint, labor's new prosperity is not without its cost.

8 THE CHALLENGES AHEAD

In the year 1234 Koreans developed the first movable metal type for printing, 200 years before the Germans "invented" it. In 1442 Koreans developed the pluviometer, or rain gauge, 200 years before the Italians "invented" it and employed farming methods unknown in the West. And in 1592, in response to a Japanese invasion, Koreans developed and built the world's first iron-clad ships, again 200 years before they were "invented" by the Americans. After centuries of external domination and exploitation, Korea is again emerging as an independent nation and, simultaneously, moving into such current technological developments as the 4MB DRAM microprocessor, advanced telecommunications, and aerospace technology. Being technologically innovative is not new for Korea.

This book has tried to explain the reasons behind successes such as these, and in order to properly understand the so-called Miracle on the Han River, it has considered not just the business environment in which Korean firms operate but also the cultural environment, since both of these factors interact to create what we call "Korean-style management." Korean history and cultural development are the backdrop to any study of Korean firms, and most of the chaebols display relatively consistent patterns of family ownership and control, centralized and paternalistic management, close business-government ties, and an entrepreneurial orientation and drive seldom seen today in the West. The four largest companies (Samsung, Hyundai, Lucky-Goldstar, and Daewoo) were discussed in detail to illustrate how such companies grew, developed, and prospered. In addition, we reviewed industrial policies in business-government relations, corporate strategies for global competition, management processes and the work environment, and human resources management and labor relations.

Many factors help explain the Korean success story—why these companies have been so successful in such a short a period of time. Several of these have to do with features commonly found in developing nations (such as low wage rates, undemanding workers, centralized power and decisionmaking, and relatively few government regulations). Even so, many underdeveloped nations in Latin America and Africa today exhibit these same features yet remain locked in poverty with little sustained economic growth. The unique blend of traditional culture and pragmatic ability to adapt to changing environmental conditions have made the difference for Korea.

To begin with, the Confucian heritage of East Asia has endowed Korea with an unsurpassed work ethic. Koreans on average work longer and harder than almost anyone else. Moreover, Koreans exist and work in a highly structured and homogeneous society, characterized by strong social pressures to conform, obey, and belong. Workers have historically demonstrated unquestioned commitment and loyalty to their employers, and the prevailing feeling is that the current generation is obliged to sacrifice its own well-being for the benefit of future generations.

Companies in many ways resemble large families in which the father figure (the manager) is to be obeyed at all costs. This practice, in turn, is reinforced by the larger Korean society, where the husband is head of the household and the husband's job and status within the company are vitally important to the family. In return for this commitment, employers are expected to look after the basic needs of employees and their families. In this system of mutual benefit and mutual obligation, everyone has a place. Add to this a strong belief in preserving group harmony and we have some idea of how the social system supported economic and corporate development.

The government has played an important role in the success of Korean firms through its industrial planning and coordination and by creating quasi-monopolistic support for the targeted companies. The government has assisted companies with essential financing for expansion, favorable tax policies, control over labor activities, acquisition of advanced scientific and manufacturing technology, and access to foreign markets. A system of mutually supportive collaborative arrangements has emerged in which the government and its ministries serve the interests of a group of selected companies by creating business opportunities, while the companies serve the interests of the government by contributing to Korea's overall economic growth and development. In other words, business, government, and to some extent the larger society work to develop a prosperous Korean economy.

Finally, these societal and governmental forces have allowed Korean companies to develop a distinctive approach to organization and management—one that has been characterized by its emphasis on corporate growth and development at almost any cost. Korean drive and ambition can be seen in the brief biographies of the chairmen of some of the major chaebols (see Chapter 4), as well as in the examples of various workers and managers discussed throughout this book. Through a combination of hard work, an entrepreneurial spirit, and an approach to human resources management that is congruent with prevailing social norms and values, Korean companies have grown and prospered in a highly competitive global marketplace.

Even so, significant changes are occurring in Korea and in other countries around the world that will influence both industrial society and industrial success in the years ahead. The rules of international trade are changing, as are the expectations and demands of the Korean people themselves, and the intersection of these two forces is going to profoundly affect Korean corporations and management. The manner in which Korean companies respond to these challenges will largely determine whether Korea becomes a global leader on the industrial scene or merely one of many players.

KOREA: TOWARD THE YEAR 2000

Before examining the challenges facing Korean corporations, it is instructive to first consider several basic societal changes that seem imminent over the next decade. By the year 2000, Korea is predicted to experience a number of fundamental changes that may decisively affect business and society (D. K. Kim 1989; Shin 1988a). According to Kim (1989, 6), Korean society in the twenty-first century "will be something like a combination of the best taken from both the East and the West." Four predicted changes are examined in this section: trends toward increased harmony, economic prosperity, personal opportunity, and academic and scientific achievement.

Increased Harmony

Although Koreans often speak of the concept of harmony, they sometimes are referring to an ideal state and not a real one—witness, for example, the recent strife between labor and management and the student riots over political democracy. Many people have argued that there is reason to believe that Korea will make increasing progress toward this ideal state and point to several initial signs of this progress. Labor relations are currently in a turbulent state, but both managers and workers are increasingly realizing that the economic growth experienced over the past two decades cannot be sustained unless real improvements are made in labor-management relations. Both sides seem committed to moving in this direction.

Moreover, political turmoil may subside as South Korea increases its democratization efforts and secures its place in the international community. Relations between the two Koreas are slowly improving, and South Korea has made progress in developing both economic and political relations with the Soviet Union and the People's Republic of China—which should lead to less friction both within Korea and between Korea and its neighbors.

Increased Economic Prosperity

In addition, Korea is expected to continue to develop as a major industrialized power (Bayard and Young 1989; Kang 1989). The Economic Planning Board of Korea estimates that per capita GNP will reach $8,016 by the end of the century, or more than twice what it was in 1987 (see Exhibit 8–1). Moreover, it is estimated that by the year 2000 Korea will be one of the top ten industrialized nations of the world (up from its current position of seventeenth). In terms of production, sales, and productivity, Korea will likely be ranked first in shipbuilding, first or second in television and VCRs, third in microchips, third in robotics, fifth in steel, and fourth or fifth in automobiles (D. K. Kim 1989). These increases probably will be accompanied by shifts in the production mix of industry, as shown in a recent study published by the Korean Institute for Economics and Technology (see Exhibit 8-2). With population and economic growth rates predicted to be relatively stable, the economic future of Korea is indeed bright.

Exhibit 8-1. The Korean Economy in the Year 2000.

	1987	1991 (estimated)	2000 (estimated)
Population (in millions)	42.3	44.1	49.4
Economic growth rate	12.0%	7.5%	6.7%
GNP ($ billion)	$111.6	$224.9	$395.9
Per capita GNP	$2,804	$5,100	$8,016
Exports ($ billion)	$47.3	$76.7	$173.2
Imports ($ billion)	$41.0	$73.3	$170.5

Source: From data supplied by the Korean Economic Planning Board and cited in D. K. Kim, "Korea Towards the Twenty-first Century," paper presented at the International Conference on Management, Honolulu, 13 January 1989.

Exhibit 8-2. Projected Changes in Industrial Production Mix, 1984–2010.

	Percent of Industrial Production	
Category of Goods	1984	2010 (projected)
Textiles	14%	6%
Machinery	11	15
Food	10	6
Electronics	10	22
Steel	8	4
Vehicles	3	10
Shipbuilding	3	1
Fine chemicals	3	6
Petrochemicals	3	2
Sports and leisure	2	2
Other	33	26
	100%	100%

Source: Korean Institute for Economics and Technology as reported in *The Economist* (May 21, 1988): 4–10.

Increased Personal Opportunity

Korea has historically been a class society. In feudal days there existed a *yangban*, or noble-scholars class, at the top of society, followed in descending order by the *ajon* (official clerks), *sangmin* (ordinary people), and *cheonmin* (humble people) classes. Farmers and merchants—including businessmen—generally belonged to the lower classes. During the past three decades, however—partly as a result of the move toward political democracy and the substantial economic progress brought on under the leadership of the chaebols— the class structure has largely disappeared. Businessmen are no longer regarded as part of a lower class—or any class, for that matter. One young stockbroker in Seoul recently observed that when he joined a brokerage firm several years ago, the profession was not entirely respectable. "Girls didn't want to go out with stockbrokers. But now we're very popular," he noted (Moffat 1989, A4). People who join the large corporations today typically are respected for their contribution to the economic development of the nation and for their self-sacrifice.

By the year 2000 this trend toward increased opportunity in various professions is expected to continue. Employment will increasingly be based on ability and not connections or family. More women can be expected to enter higher positions within the organizations, and promotion within the organizational hierarchy will increasingly be based on merit and performance instead of seniority. In short, there will be a move toward professionalism in management.

Increased Academic and Scientific Achievement

Korea has been described as an academic society. Confucian principles supporting the importance of learning have existed for centuries, and as noted earlier, Korea has one of the highest literacy rates in the world (significantly higher than that of the United States). Even so, the trend toward more and better education will probably increase, not decrease. Korea is currently producing about 32,000 applied science graduates each year. Proportionately, this is far more than the numbers produced in the United States and about the same as in

Japan. Because status and opportunity in Korea are influenced by academic credentials, no change is foreseen here.

Increasing amounts of money are also being invested in basic and applied research both by corporations and by the government (see Chapter 4). In the not-too-distant future, this country of 40 plus million (with a GNP about equal to Denmark's) will likely emerge as one of the world's foremost scientific think tanks, especially in fields of advanced technology. Korea has a real commitment to technological advancement and the will to succeed in this endeavor. As Kumho's President Park put it during a recent interview, "The Korean people have a higher need to achieve than anyone I know."

In fact, one Japanese futurist, Dr. Sha Seiki, recently published a book entitled *The Reasons Why Japan Will Surpass the U.S.A. and Korea Will Surpass Japan*, in which he argues that by the year 2010 Korea will actually surpass Japan in economic development (see D. K. Kim 1989 for discussion). First, according to Dr. Seiki, if present population trends continue, by the year 2010 two-thirds of the Japanese will be over thirty-five, while two-thirds of the Koreans will be under thirty-five. Japan will emerge as "a country of old people," while Korea will be "a country of young people."

Second, Seiki claims that Japanese youth are becoming increasingly "decadent" (compared to Koreans) as their affluence increases and their drive for achievement decreases. This prediction basically says that Japan will go the way of the United States: Increasing prosperity will corrupt the nation's youth. Recent observations seem to confirm this trend in Japan, but the same malady may occur in Korea as it becomes more prosperous.

Third, every young Korean male must serve in the military for three years, which seems to instill a greater sense of patriotism, dedication, and mission in Koreans than in their Japanese counterparts. Fourth, Dr. Seiki asserts that Koreans are more individualistic, more creative, and more committed to academic achievement than the Japanese and, fifth, that Korea's history of adversity motivates Koreans to work harder to succeed. This is clearly a relative statement, however, because the Japanese also have experienced adversity and work quite hard. Seiki's point here is that the Koreans will work harder. A case in point is the change in some Korean corporate slogans from "Let's catch up with Japan" to "Let's Surpass Japan." Finally, it is argued that the Koreans will surpass Japan because they simply do things faster. It took the United States 100 years to move from an agrarian state to an industrialized economy, and it took Japan seventy years to make a similar adjustment, but it took Korea less than thirty years.

Certainly not everyone agrees with these projections or conclusions. In fact, some might take issue with the data themselves. Even so, the point here is not whether Korea will overtake Japan—Japan will not stand still. Instead, the point is that by any measure Korea is on the move and its rate of development is proceeding at a pace that far exceeds the rate of many industrialized countries, including the United States. In short, Korea must be recognized as an economic power for the future.

CHALLENGES FACING KOREAN CORPORATIONS TODAY

In view of these changes emerging in Korean society, challenges lay ahead for contemporary Korean firms. If these firms are to continue to grow and prosper, they must find a way to adapt to these societal changes, as well as other changes—and challenges—occurring throughout the world. Indeed, it is a time of decision for the chaebols.

The Economic Challenge

Despite significant economic progress—indeed, partly because of it—Korea today faces increased challenges on the economic front. From a macro-economic standpoint, it needs to maintain a high growth rate so that economic development continues. However, tension is increasing between Korea and its trading partners (especially the United States and Western Europe) over the trade imbalances brought on by Korean economic success. The United States currently has a $9 billion annual trade deficit with Korea, and Western governments have moved toward increased protectionism.

In addition, many countries accuse Korea (with good reason) of failing to open its markets to foreign products and competition. Indeed, when the Korean government reluctantly reduced some trade barriers (as it did for tobacco, movies, and some farm products), "popular"—that is, highly organized—protests and boycotts were initiated until the government relaxed its efforts. Such short-sighted practices by special interest groups in Korea create additional tensions and increase the probability of overt actions by others. In the last six years, between 35 and 45 percent of Korean exports have come under some form of foreign restriction, and this trend is likely to increase unless serious corrective actions are taken within Korea. To the extent that protectionism diminishes and a more open market economy emerges, Korean companies will face an increasing need for professional managers to meet the growing competition.

At home, there is a need to further develop internal markets and satisfy the increased consumer demands of a more prosperous society. Korea has a growing middle class that is anxious to see the fruits of its labor, and to a large extent, political stability in the future rests with the government's ability to fulfill these expectations.

Throughout the expansion of both their internal and external markets, Korean corporations will have to find new ways to secure the necessary financing for growth because government-controlled sources have diminished. Korean companies are highly leveraged (with high debt-equity ratios), which puts many in precarious financial positions. Daewoo, for example, recently had to appeal for government help for its financially troubled shipbuilding company. As the government moves toward more open capital markets, requiring corporations to be more competitive in their financial transactions (Sanchez 1989), the firms are experiencing considerable pressure to become better managers of their financial resources. As part of this process, an increasing distinction is likely to be evident between owners and managers as a true stock market emerges.

The Political Challenge

Much has been written concerning recent political changes throughout Korea, and although politics is not the focus of this book, these changes have significantly affected the chaebols. In essence, the move toward democratization has greatly diminished—although certainly not destroyed—the power and influence of the "old boy's network" between corporate executives and high-ranking government officials. Such relations will of necessity continue to be a central aspect of doing business in Korea, but the previous intimacy between these two groups will be less evident.

As the government distances itself from perceptions or accusations of corporate favoritism, the once cozy business-government relations already have become somewhat strained, and this development has had positive and negative consequences for both sides. For the government, close ties to industry in the past have greatly facilitated efficient growth and development (see Chapter 2), and the severance of many of these ties means that government now loses some of its influence in corporate decisions about industrial development. Government will offer less indicative planning and less help for distressed industries. In short, there will be some movement toward a freer market with fewer controls, a change that already has been seen in the insurance and airline industries. For the corporations, the loss of some of these close ties with government means reduced access to readily available financing for future projects and increased difficulties in hurdling governmental bureaucratic barriers for new ventures.

Even so, the new political climate and its resulting revised contract between business and government also mean less government-sanctioned corruption (as in the case of the Kukje Group) and more efficiency through increased competition. It is also beneficial for small and medium-sized companies and subcontractors that in the past have often found themselves excluded from competition by the major firms. The changes also mean that companies in the future will have to rely increasingly on professional managers to skillfully guide them through the new industrial competitiveness.

The Technological Challenge

Korea faces an increasingly complex technological environment. It has found it relatively easy to acquire aging technology (sometimes through joint ventures, sometimes through reverse-engineering) and compete on the international marketplace based on product price. This is largely how Korean companies entered markets like consumer electronics, automobiles, and household appliances. Today, however, as the half-life of technology-based products declines and as labor costs escalate, it has become increasingly important for Korean companies to develop their own technology and be first to market. This puts these companies squarely in competition with American, Japanese, and European companies that have far more resources to devote to research and development.

Korea's answer to date has been a combination of leading-edge joint ventures with both Japanese and Western companies that either have or are developing the required technologies and individual or consortium efforts within Korea to create what is needed. An example of the former strategy of joint ventures is Goldstar's telecommunications efforts in concert with North American partners, while an example of the latter strategy can be seen in the development of the 4MB DRAM chip described in Chapter 5. In both cases, the stakes are high. Over the next five years, the country's largest chaebols will collectively invest more than $1.3 billion to develop state-of-the-art microprocessors, VCRs, and advanced telecommunications equipment. This represents a huge investment for a country the size of Korea, yet it is small compared to the $28 billion Japan will spend during the same period. For Korea to remain competitive, this investment is only the beginning.

The Human Resource Challenge

Finally, changes that are occurring in Korean society also are affecting labor-management relations and the nature of human resource management. As noted in Chapter 7, employees at all levels are increasingly demanding a greater share of the benefits of the emerging economic prosperity. The new movement toward political democracy has fueled demands for workplace democracy, with greater worker autonomy and participation. Strike activity has greatly increased, as have turnover rates. Commitment to the company, once assumed, is now seen as diminishing, and workers are demanding greater input in corporate decisions: They want works councils that have real substance. In short, Korea has reached the stage of rising entitlements, where people feel they deserve more. Such is the nature of successful economic development.

In the increasingly competitive business environment facing companies today (with fewer government guarantees, more competition, higher labor costs, and so forth), a company's human resources become a vital asset. However, just when Korean companies need this asset most, labor's commitment remains unclear. Hence, a major challenge facing contemporary firms in Korea is how to negotiate a new social contract that is acceptable to its workforce at all levels of the organization. This new social contract must effectively deal with the needs and expectations of the members of the organization in such a way that harmony is restored and broad-based support for the company and its goals is achieved. If Korean managers have a difficult task for the future, this is surely it.

IMPLICATIONS FOR KOREAN MANAGEMENT

In order to meet these challenges, Korean companies must adapt their management styles. Strategies and structures must also be modified where necessary to accommodate the new realities (Y. K. Shin 1988a). These changes can be seen in five areas of management concern (see Exhibit 8-3). Variations on these themes can be found, but the following predictions can be made concerning future changes in Korean management:

1. *Management control: from owners to professional managers.* Because of the political move toward democratization and decentralization and because of the economic shifts requiring competitive skills, control of the major chaebols will continue to evolve toward control by professional managers instead of owners or family members. This trend will be somewhat accelerated by the increasing age or death of the original founders who once ruled with tight controls. In some of the chaebols, such as the Lotte Group, none of the founder's sons wish to be involved in the business. Because of these

Exhibit 8-3. Predicted Changes in the Management Style of Korean Companies.

Characteristic	From	Toward
Management control	Owner control	Professional management
Corporate strategy	Random growth and diversification	Strategic and incremental development
Corporate culture	People-oriented	People and efficiency
Human resource management	Seniority	Seniority and merit
Labor relations	Authoritarianism	Cooperation

Source: Based on Y. K. Shin, "Changes in Society and Management in Korea," paper presented at symposium jointly sponsored by Korean Chamber of Commerce and Industry and the Korean Academy of Management, Seoul, 28 October 1988.

changes, increasing reliance on well-trained professional managers will become a hallmark of many Korean firms.

2. *Corporate strategy: from random growth and diversification to strategic and incremental development.* Korean corporations will increasingly focus on growth and development through logical incrementalism. That is, whereas in the past companies moved into new business based on hunches or random opportunity and often grew unwieldy as a result (called the "octopus strategy"), the emphasis will be to develop more refined business lines and focus developmental efforts within these areas. This is not to say that unique opportunities will not be explored; rather, the general trend will more than likely be that the chaebols will become more conservative in their corporate strategies and tend to focus on their core businesses. In view of increased competition, increased R&D expenditures, and decreased government support and guarantees, this is simply a wise course of action.

3. *Corporate culture: from concern for people to concern for people and efficiency.* Korea's Confucian heritage has led to the creation of corporations in which mutual commitments between employees and employer were preeminent. In the pursuit of harmony, employers had a responsibility to take care of their people, and employees had a duty to show respect and obedience to management. Again, as a result of recent political and economic changes, this traditional system is breaking down. What in the past was seen as acceptable paternalism is now often seen by some as unacceptable authoritarianism and exploitation. Moreover, in the drive to be competitive, managers are under increasing pressure to view employees as part of the production process instead of as a member of the corporate family. As a result of these forces, increasing emphasis is being placed on ensuring efficiency and productivity on the shop floor. Concern for people is present, but it now has to share center stage with increasing concerns for effectiveness.

4. *Human resource management: from seniority to seniority and merit.* Again because of societal changes and increased competition, Korean companies are moving tentatively toward a greater focus on employee performance and merit as a basis for reward, promotion, and retention. The "whole man" concept is still important in such decisions, but Korean managers are showing less willingness to tolerate mistakes or consistently mediocre performance. Change can be seen at the margins, where extremely good performers move up the

corporate hierarchy at a faster pace than their coworkers and relatively poor performers are removed with increasing regularity. For those in the middle, the change is less severe.

5. *Labor relations: from authoritarianism to increased cooperation.* The final change to be seen in Korean management concerns labor relations. Because of recent labor turmoil, new government support for unionization, and reduced power of the chaebol leaders, a moderate shift is occurring away from autocratic management toward a more participative style. A major vehicle for accomplishing this is through the more effective utilization of the existing works councils, combined with renewed emphasis on human relations training for managers. The concept of paternalistic management has not disappeared, nor will it. It is still the responsibility of the company to look after employees. However, the nature and quality of this paternalism is being modified in order to recognize the increasing maturity and capabilities of subordinates. Commitment to the organization will still be encouraged but will rest more on the principle of mutual benefit than on mutual obligation.

Hence, the emerging Korean management style will resemble somewhat more closely what we are familiar with in the West. However, it would be a mistake to describe this as Western-style management. Instead, the new management will be highly pragmatic, adopting new techniques from different sources and modifying them to meet the unique cultural and environmental demands, and throughout this evolutionary process, the traditional values that have defined Korean culture and business enterprise for centuries will play a central role. The new Korea will not abandon or forget the old.

LESSONS FOR THE WEST

The final question we wish to address is what the West can learn from the Korean experience. Korea has learned much from the West over the past several decades; it has seen the West as a repository of information to be tapped. As countries around the world increasingly recognize the trend toward globalization of business, perhaps managers in the West might consider what we, in turn, can learn from Korea. While it is always difficult to generalize and while exceptions can always be found, we nevertheless suggest that Western managers at least consider the following:

1. *We need to rediscover the entrepreneurial spirit.* To the external observer, a key feature that distinguishes a typical Korean company from its Western counterpart is its unbridled drive for achievement and success. Korean firms exhibit considerably greater entrepreneurial spirit, hard work, and tenacity than firms in North America or Europe. Their executives are consistently looking for new opportunities or ways to improve on old opportunities. Korean executives are often criticized for their overly zealous approach to work, but positive results reinforce this behavior. If the average American manager works forty-five hours per week, and his Korean counterpart works seventy, it should be obvious who will accomplish more.

In addition to hours of work, Koreans have a sense of urgency in developing their businesses; they are forever looking for ways to improve the product, the marketing plan, the pricing structure, and so forth. Americans, by contrast, all too often seem to believe in leaving the business alone unless an observable problem arises ("Don't fix it if it isn't broken."). Under this strategy, by the time a problem is clearly recognizable, it may be too late to save the business from the competition. A primary lesson for the West is the need to rekindle the entrepreneurial spirit in such a way that its managers become more imaginative, more innovative, and more competitive.

2. *We need to respond rapidly and intelligently to environmental changes and challenges.* Managers and companies in the West need to pay more attention to environmental shifts and move quickly to adapt to them. All too often, Western managers respond to market changes either through appeals for legislative protectionism or through efforts to change the market instead of the product. Changing the company's way of doing business or its products is often the last thing considered. Europe's response to a threatened market is often to erect trade barriers, while simultaneously denying they are doing so. The United States often appears to ignore the problem altogether.

Consider two recent examples from Japan. When U.S. automobile makers are asked how they intend to sell more cars in Japan (where cars are driven on the left side of the road), a typical response is that the Japanese need to be convinced to change to the right side of the road like the Americans. Thus, U.S. cars do not need changing—only the highways of Japan. Similarly, a delegation of lumber producers from the United States was recently sent to Japan to convince homebuilders there to convert to "feet and inches" instead of their traditional measures because U.S. mills were already set up for this. Such nearsighted efforts to change or limit the market only provide excuses for failure instead of opportunities for success. The Koreans have been adept at sensing and coping with environmental changes, whether in the marketplace or in the workplace.

3. *We need to develop a long-term orientation and commitment.* A third lesson derives not only from Korea but also from Japan. Koreans, like the Japanese, believe in long-term commitments, which applies to decisions about product development and market entry and to interpersonal relationships. In contrast, all too often the West enters short-term market ventures and relies on promotional materials instead of people in its business dealings. Sales representatives are moved around frequently and pass their old customers on to new (and unknown) representatives in the process. As a result, Westerners do not get to know the people they do business with and thus feel no commitment to continue working for a particular firm. If there is a lesson here, it is the need for companies to develop a long-term perspective in their approach to business. In view of the cultural differences between Eastern and Western societies, clearly some compromise is in order here. Americans probably will never demonstrate the longevity in business relations found in the East, but they might hope for at least modest extensions of their field of vision.

4. *We need to plan more systematically.* Korean companies do an exceedingly good job of environmental scanning. They collect considerable information from various sources, cross-check the accuracy of the information, and then use what they learn to develop long-range plans and objectives. It was noted in Chapter 3 that most chaebols have central planning offices that report directly to the chairman. Thus, quality information is used at the highest levels where long-range planning occurs. Once plans are established, corporate resources are marshalled to facilitate goal accomplishment.

In the United States, planning efforts tend to be diffused throughout the organization, leading to reduced synergy, lost information, and often reduced importance or input in the organizational decision-making process for managers. On a per capita basis, Western firms spend considerably more than their Korean counterparts on information gathering and planning. However, the return on investment for such expenditures is often much lower.

5. *We need to better use our human resources.* Concerns in the West all too often focus on discovering ways to better *control* employees instead of ways to better *use* them. Despite rhetoric to the contrary, the typical U.S. firm tends to view its human resources as an expensive—and often expendable—cost in the production process. As such, the "responsible" manager looks for ways to minimize these costs where possible, either through increased automation, layoffs for temporarily idle workers, job fractionization, or other such means. Such practices send a clear signal to employees about their lack of importance to the organization. It is also a significant waste of valuable talent. Unfortunately, short-sighted labor union practices in the West often exacerbate the problem by opposing innovations that could contribute to increased efficiency and by failing to take the initiative with management in developing a common sense of purpose. Both management and labor can be blamed for our current economic malady.

Added to this problem in many companies is a frequent management attitude that employees cannot be trusted to manage their own affairs. Books like *The One-Minute Manager* sell well in the West because they all too often view the management process as one of providing short, quick, and impersonal feedback to employees to control their behavior and "keep them on track." The thought of developing a deeper understanding of employee needs and goals or of how each employee could potentially contribute to the organization seldom occurs to Westerners, who tend to manage "by the numbers." Koreans tend to manage by results. There is a big difference between the two methods. Although clearly far from perfect, Korean managers and firms spend more time selecting new employees and, once employees are hired, make a greater effort to treat employees like colleagues in a joint endeavor. Managers get to know their subordinates and frequently try to the best of their ability to develop a team spirit within the group. Emotional bonds and mutual commitments develop that serve the interests of both the employees and the corporation. Although some Western firms also do this, their number is not large.

6. *We need to develop more productive business-government relations.* In the United States it is commonly assumed that business and government are and probably should be adversaries. The government's role is to ensure fair and open competition and to be ever vigilant in the pursuit of rule-breakers. Business, on the other hand, is

expected to pursue stockholder interests at almost any cost, hopefully within prescribed legal limits. Clearly, this adversarial relationship has not worked. U.S. business spends too much time dealing with government regulations, fighting hostile takeovers, and pursuing paper profits and far too little time actually making products. Research and development efforts tend to focus on short-term applications of existing technologies, and market research often invests too much time considering ways to create artificial demand for products that lack substance. Managers focus on developing their careers and not their companies. Meanwhile, government continues to develop its bureaucracies, rules, and power base with little consideration for how it could really facilitate industrial competitiveness. A case in point here can be seen in the recent savings and loan association debacle. This industry has lost billions of dollars (which American taxpayers are expected to repay), yet it is already one of the most regulated industries in the country. Clearly, government regulations failed to encourage an efficient—let alone honest—industry.

Despite past abuses of power by government, various Korean ministries have made strenuous efforts to assist business growth and national economic development. The sense of oneness of purpose as business and government worked together for the common good has been similar to that found in Japan. Although the specific model used in Korea (or Japan) is clearly inappropriate for the United States, the basic notion of government as a partner with business—instead of an adversary—is certainly worth considering by Western political leaders committed to economic growth and competitiveness.

Hence, as we close this analysis of the strategy and structure of Korean firms, we are left with the conclusion that not only is Korea a country on the move but that perhaps the West can learn something useful from the Korean experience. Certainly there are cultural differences between the two societies, and each has its own geopolitical and economic agendas. Even so, Korea has for many years been a good student of the West, and perhaps the time has come now for us to return to school. By learning more about this and other countries, we may discover new ways to improve our own competitiveness in the global environment, and in the process we can learn more about the culture, accomplishments, and dreams of an important ally. Korea has been a good student; perhaps now it can emerge as a good teacher.

Throughout the turbulent history of Korea, two leaders stand out for universal recognition and praise. The first is King Sejong, the fifteenth-century renaissance ruler who encouraged the development of science and technology, education, and cultural development. This scholarly monarch oversaw a period of sustained economic and intellectual enrichment whose influence continues to this day. The other leader is Admiral Yi Sun-sin, the sixteenth-century military commander who exhibited both the unyielding determination and the cunning strategy to defeat successive Japanese military invasions of Korea. The Korean people are very proud of these two leaders because of their drive, intellect, tenacity, and success. And, by the same token, one cannot help but think that these two leaders would be very proud of the Korean people today, since their legacies continue to thrive in contemporary Korean industrial society.

REFERENCES

Abegglen, James, and George Stalks. 1985. *Kaisha: The Japanese Corporation*. New York: Harper & Row.

Asia Week. 1988. Korea's Striking Improvement. 15 July, 53.

Bae C. S. 1988. Sunkyong Group: Making Profits the Clean Way. *Business Korea*, December, 25–30.

Bae Joon. 1985. The New Division Commanders of the Seven Chaebol Groups. *Sin-Dong-A*, April, 524–48.

———. 1986. "Ex-Bureaucrats and Ex-Military Men in the Financial World." *Sin-Dong-A*, August, 403.

Bae Kyuhan. 1987. *Automobile Workers in Korea*. Seoul: Korea: Seoul National University Press.

Bae Kyuhan, and William Form. 1986. Payment Strategy in South Korea's Advanced Economic Sector. *American Sociological Review*, February, 120–31.

Bank of Korea. 1989. Base Year Adjustment of GNP Statistics by Bank of Korea. *Korean Central Daily*, 1 March, p. 1.

Baum, Laurie. 1987. Korea's Newest Export: Management Style. *Business Week*, 19 January, 66.

Bayard, Thomas O., and Soo-Gil Young. 1989. *Economic Relations between the United States and Korea: Conflict or Cooperation?* Washington, D.C.: Institute for International Economics.

Business Korea. 1986. Womanpower: Unsung Praises. September, 20–25.

_____ . 1987. Samsung Group: Aftermath of Lee's Death. December, 46–49.

_____ . 1988a. Asiana Airlines: International Flair and Korean Heart. December, 42.

_____ . 1988b. Birth of an Airline (Kumho). April, 90.

_____ . 1988c. Daewoo Shipbuilding and Heavy Machinery: Begging Political Pardon. December, 31.

_____ . 1988d. Hyundai's Sonata: Creating a New Consumption Pattern. October, 46–47.

_____ . 1988e. Samsung After 50 Years: New Leadership Amid Changing Times. March, 25–40.

_____ . 1988f. Samsung's Lee Kun Hee: Giving Big Business a New Role. December, 15.

_____ . 1988g. Sunkyong Corporate Structure: An Informal Approach to Success. December, 29–30.

Business Week. 1987. Will Labor Unrest Wreck the Boom? 31 August, 12.

Caulkin, Simon. 1986. Why Daewoo Works Harder. *Management Today*, July, 62–67, 100.

Chang Chan Sup. 1987. Management of Chaebol: The Conglomerate in South Korea. *Proceedings of the 1987 Pan Pacific Conference*, Taipei, Taiwan, 42–47.

Charters, Ann. 1984. Daewoo: Turning Point for a South Korean Giant. *Financial Times*, 31 October, 16–17.

Choi Jang Jip. 1983. *Interest Conflict and Political Control in South Korea: A Study of the Labor Unions in Manufacturing Industries: 1961–1980*. University of Chicago, Ph.D. dissertation.

Clifford, Mark. 1987. Labor Strikes Out. *Far Eastern Economic Review*, 27 August, 14–19.

_____ . 1988a. Filing for Divorce (Kukje). *Far Eastern Economic Review*, 21 April, 58–60.

_____ . 1988b. Labor Striking at the Heart. *Far Eastern Economic Review*, 24 March, 106.

_____ . 1988c. A Lifeboat for Daewoo. *Far Eastern Economic Review*, 8 December, 52–56.

_____ . 1988d. Samsung Under Siege. *Far Eastern Economic Review*, 15 December, 104.

_____ . 1989. Fledgling Airline Breaks KAL's Monopoly. *Far Eastern Economic Review*, 2 February, 24.

_____ . 1989. Sonata at Hyundai. *Far Eastern Economic Review*, 2 February, 56.

Clifford, Mark, and Jonathan Moore. 1989. Squeezed by Success. *Far Eastern Economic Review*, 16 March, 84–89.

Cooper, Nancy. 1987. South Korea: Labor Pains. *Newsweek*, 31 August, 20–21.

Crane, Paul S. 1978. *Korean Patterns*. Seoul: Kwangjin Publishing Co.

Daewoo Corporation, Education and Training Dept., Planning and Coordination Division. 1984. *Education and Training at Daewoo*. Seoul.

Daewoo Group. 1987a. *Annual Report*. Seoul.

_____. 1987b. *Daewoo Corporation*. Seoul.

_____. 1987c. *Daewoo Shipbuilding and Heavy Machinery, Ltd*. Seoul.

_____. 1988a. *Daewoo Corporation*. Seoul.

_____. 1988b. *News from Daewoo*. Seoul.

DeMente, Boye. 1988. *Korean Etiquette and Business Ethics in Business*. Lincolwood, Ill.: NTC Business Books.

Dong A. Ilbo. 2 May, 1984.

Doosan Group. 1986. *The Doosan Group*. Seoul.

Dreyfuss, Joel. 1987. South Korea's Days of Danger. *Fortune*, 26 October, 66–69.

The Economist. 1988a. The Economist's Survey of South Korea. 21 May, 1–22.

_____. 1988b. South Korea: Contentment Has Its Price. 23 July, 34.

_____. 1989. Memory Chips Welcome Korea. 4 February, 66.

England, George W. 1967. Personal Value Systems of American Managers. *Academy of Management Journal* 10 (Spring): 53–68.

Far Eastern Economic Review. 1988. Under-Powered Performer (Daewoo). 8 December, 52–53.

_____. 1989. Goldstar to Build TV Plant in China. 2 February, 63.

Forbes. 1988. Samsung: South Korea Marches to a Different Drummer. 16 May, 84–89.

Fortune. 1988. The Fortune International 500. 1 August, D1–D36.

Haitai Group. 1987. *Haitai Group of Companies*. Seoul.

Halberstram, David. 1986. *The Reckoning*. New York: William Morrow.

Hanjin Group. 1987. *Korean Air—Annual Report 1987*. Seoul.

_____. 1988. *The Hanjin Group—Company Report*. Seoul.

Hattori Tamio. 1984. Ownership and Management of Modern Korean Corporations. *Azia Keizai* (Asian Economy, in Japanese), May–June, 37–53.

_____. 1986. Comparison of Large Corporations in Korea and Japan. In *The Structure and Strategy of Korean Corporations* (in Korean), ed. Hakjon Lee and Kuhyun Chung, 172–189. Seoul: Bupmunsa.

Ho Davis Yau-Fai. 1976. On the Concept of Face. *American Journal of Sociology* 81 (Winter): 867–84.

Hofstede, Geert, and Michael Harris Bond. 1988. The Confucius Connection: From Cultural Roots to Economic Growth. *Organizational Dynamics* (Spring): 5–21.

Hurst, G. Cameron. 1984. Getting a Piece of the ROK: American Problems Doing Business in Korea. Hanover, N.H.: Universities Field Staff International Reports.

Hyundai Group. 1985. *Hyundai News.* Seoul.

_____ . 1986a. *Annual Report.* Seoul.

_____ . 1986b. *Hyundai Heavy Industries Company, Ltd.* Seoul.

_____ . 1986c. *Hyundai in Brief.* Seoul.

_____ . 1986d. *Introducing Hyundai.* Seoul.

Jang Song-Hyon. 1988. *The Key to Successful Business in Korea.* Seoul: Yong Ahn.

Japanese Ministry of Labor. 1986. The Japanese Work Week. Tokyo, 1986.

Johnson, Chalmers, ed. 1984. *The Industrial Policy Debate.* San Francisco: Institute for Contemporary Studies.

Kang T. W. 1989. *Is Korea the Next Japan?* New York: Free Press.

Kia Motors. 1987a. *Annual Report.* Seoul.

_____ . 1987b. *Road to the Future.* Seoul.

Kim Dong Ki. 1985. Cultural Aspects of Higher Productivity. In *Toward Higher Productivity: Experiences of the Republic of Korea*, ed. D. K. Kim. Tokyo: Asian Productivity Organization.

_____ . 1989. Korea Towards the Twenty-first Century. Paper presented at the International Conference on Management, Honolulu, 13 January.

Kim Jin Moon, and Sung Won Shim. 1988. Kumho Group: From Tires to Fliers in a Single Bound. *Business Korea*, April, 29–36.

Kim Kyong-Dong. 1985. *Man and Society in Korea's Economic Growth.* Seoul: Seoul National University Press.

_____ . 1987. Koreans: Who Are They? In *Doing Business in Korea*, ed. Arthur Whitehill, 7–17. London: Croom Helm.

Kim Soo Kon. 1987. "Labour and Employment." In *Doing Business in Korea*, ed. Arthur M. Whitehill, 39–56. London: Croom Helm.

Kim Woo-Choong. 1983. Cited in DeMente 1988, 35–36.

_____ . 1988. *Daewoo's Story: The Realization of Entrepreneurship.* Speech delivered at the Fifth Annual ACE-YEO International Conference, Washington, D.C., 5 March.

Kim Yung-Chung. 1976. *Women of Korea: A History from Ancient Times to 1945.* Seoul: Ewha Woman's University Press.

Kolon Group. 1987. *Annual Report.* Seoul.

Korea Explosives Group. 1988. *Korea Explosives Group: 1987/1988.* (Company Report). Seoul.

Korean Development Bank. 1984. *Annual Report.* Seoul.

Korean Herald. 1988. POSCO: World's Most Advanced Steel Mill. 13 July, 1–3.

Kraar, Louis. 1987. Kim Woo-Chung: Korea's Export King. *Fortune*, 5 January, 74.

Kumho Group. 1987. *Today at Kumho Group.* Seoul.

_____ . 1988a. *Kumho.* Seoul.

_____ . 1988b. *Kumho Petrochemical Company, Ltd.* Seoul.

Lee. Byung-Chull. 1987. *The Three Crises of Samsung: A Founder's Tale.* Excerpted in *World Executive's Digest.* May, 38–56.

Lee Byung Jong. 1988a. Exporting Electronics to Japan. *Business Korea*, June, 21–23.

———. 1988b. Lotte's Shin: The Fourth Richest Man in the World. *Business Korea*, October, 67–68.

Lee Keum Hyun. 1988. Workers' Movement: No Longer a Silent Partner. *Business Korea*, December, 66–75.

Lie, John. 1988. The Ssangyong Group: An Introductory Survey of a Korean Conglomerate. *Asian Profile*, December, 487–99.

Lucky-Goldstar Group. 1985. *Annual Report.* Seoul.

———. 1986a. *Annual Review.* Seoul.

———. 1986b. *Lucky-Goldstar.* Seoul.

———. 1987a. *Company Report.* Seoul.

———. 1987b. *Lucky.* Seoul.

———. 1987c. *Lucky-Goldstar 1987.* Seoul.

———. 1988. *Goldstar.* Seoul.

Magaziner, Ira, and Mark Patinkin. 1989. Fast Heat: How Korea Won the Microwave War. *Harvard Business Review* (January–February): 83–92.

Matsumoto, K. 1986. The Chaebol: Dynamic Management. *Journal of Japanese Trade and Industry* (March–April): 2: 21.

McBeth, John. 1989. Labor Rocks the Boat. *Far Eastern Economic Review*, 5 January, 65.

Moffat, Susan. 1989. Korea Is Urgently Seeking Cheaper Credit. *Wall Street Journal*, 27 January, A-4.

Moskowitz, Karl. 1987. Korean Management Style Isn't What It Appears to Be. *Asian Wall Street Journal*, 9 March, 1.

Nakarmi, Laxmi. 1988. Korean Labor's New Voice Is Saying 'More.' *Business Week*, 2 May, 45–46.

———. 1989. It's Time for the Main Bout: Roh vs. Labor. *Business Week*, 10 April, 45–46.

Neuberger, Hugh. 1983. Business-Government Relations. Instructional Materials published by the Japan Society of New York.

Newsweek. 1988. The Pacific Century. 22 February, 42–58.

Ohmae Kenichi. 1982. *The Mind of the Strategist.* New York: McGraw-Hill.

Pohang Iron and Steel Co. 1987. *Company Report.* Seoul.

Porter, Michael. 1980. *Competitive Strategy.* New York: Free Press.

———. 1985. *Competition in Global Industries.* Cambridge, Mass.: Harvard Graduate School of Business Administration.

Register Guard. 1989. U.S. Teenagers Last in Math, Tests Show. 1 February.

Rhee Yang Soo. 1985. A Cross-Cultural Comparison of Korean and American Managerial Styles: An Inventory of Propositions. In *Administrative Dynamics and Development: The Korean Experience*, ed. B. W. Kim, D. S. Bell, and C. B. Lee. Seoul: Kyobo Publishing Co.

Rhee Yang Soo, B. Ross-Larsen, and G. Pursell. 1984. *Korea's Competitive Edge.* Baltimore: The John Hopkins University Press.

Roy, Barun. 1985. Daewoo's Kim Woo Choong: The Sky is the Limit in Perfection. *Asian Finance*, 15 November, 63–65.

Samsung Group. 1985. *Samsung: Its Role and Activities as a General Trading Company.* Seoul.

_____. 1986a. *Annual Report—1986.* Seoul.

_____. 1986b. *Samsung: Its Supplies and Services.* Seoul.

_____. 1986c. *Samsung Today.* Seoul.

_____. 1988. *Samsung, Ltd.: Financial Statements 1987.* Seoul.

Sanchez, Jesus. 1989. Asian Firms Hope to Raise Their Profiles Among American Consumers. *Los Angeles Times*, 30 January, p. IV-3.

Shim Sung Won. 1988. Pohang Iron and Steel Company: The Days of the Steel Giant. *Business Korea*, April, 49–51.

Shin Yoo Keun. 1985. *Structure and Problems in Korean Enterprises.* Seoul: Seoul National University Press.

_____. 1988a. The Changes in Society and Management in Korea. Paper presented at a symposium sponsored by the Korean Chamber of Commerce and the Korean Academy of Management, Seoul, 28 October.

_____. 1988b. Corporate Culture in Korea: The Nature and Outlook. Paper presented at the 1988 Shin Dong—a symposium on management, 15 December.

_____. 1988c. Human Resources Management in Korea. Paper presented at the Tenth International Conference of the Korean Personnel Management Association, Seoul, 21 May.

Shorrock, Tim. 1986. Growing Sunset City Attracts High-Tech, Military and Goldstar. *Business Korea*, February, 32–36.

Shrader, Erwin. 1986. Korean Manpower: Onward and Upward. *Business Korea*, September, 16–18.

Son Kil Seung. 1988. Personal communication.

Ssangyong Group. 1987. *This Is Ssangyong.* Seoul.

Steers, Richard M., and Edwin A. Miller. 1988. Management in the 1990s: The International Challenge. *Academy of Management Executive*, February, 21–22.

Steinberg, David I. 1989. *The Republic of Korea: Economic Transformation and Social Change.* Boulder, Collo.: Westview Press.

Suh, P. W. 1986. Cited in Shorrock, Tim, 1986.

Sullivan, Kevin. 1988. Japanese Success Attracts a Challenge. *Asian Business*, January, 14–16.

Sunkyong Group, Office of the Chairman for Management and Planning. 1975. *Management*. Seoul.

_____. 1986. *Sunkyong Management System*. Seoul.

_____. 1987. *Outline of Human Resources Management*. Seoul.

_____. 1988. *Looking Ahead*. Seoul.

Ungson, Gerardo R. 1990. *Competitive Strategies in High Technology*. Lexington, Mass.: D. C. Heath.

Vroom, Victor, and Phillip Yetton. 1973. *Leadership and Decision Making*. Pittsburg: University of Pittsburg Press.

Weber, Max. 1947. *The Theory of Social and Economic Organization*. New York: Free Press.

Wright, Rebecca. 1987. *Guide to Investing and Managing in South Korea*. Working Paper, College of Business, Virginia Polytechnic Institute and State University, Blacksburg, Va.

Woronoff, Jon. 1986. *Asia's "Miracle" Economies*. Tokyo: The Lotus Press, 1986.

Yates, Ronald E. 1985. How Daewoo Became a Global Giant in Just 17 Years. *Chicago Tribune*, 20 October, sec. 7, p. 25.

Yoo Sangjin, and Sang M. Lee. 1987. Management Style and Practice of Korean Chaebols. *California Management Review* (Summer): 95–110.

Yoffie, David B., and Salorio, Eugene M. 1986. South Korea: Trade and the Electronics Industry, case 387–036. Boston: Harvard Business School.

INDEX

157

ABOUT THE AUTHORS

Richard M. Steers is a professor of management in the Graduate School of Management at the University of Oregon. He holds a Ph.D. from the University of California, Irvine, and is the author of twelve books and over sixty research articles on topics ranging from employee motivation and cross-cultural management to organizational effectiveness. He is a past-president and fellow of the Academy of Management and a fellow of both the American Psychological Association and the American Psychological Society. He has served on the editorial boards of *Administrative Science Quarterly, Academy of Management Journal, Academy of Management Review*, and the *Journal of Business Research.* Prior to completing his doctorate, Professor Steers served on the corporate industrial relations staff of the Dow Chemical Company. He has also served as visiting professor at Oxford University; Nijenrode, The Netherlands School of Business; and at the University of California, Irvine.

Yoo Keun Shin is professor of management in the School of Management at Seoul National University. He received his MBA from Indiana University and his Ph.D. from Seoul National University. Professor Shin has authored seven books and numerous articles on such topics as corporate culture, management, labor relations, and business-government relations in Korean firms. Among these is the classic book, *Structure and Problems in Korean Enterprises* (Seoul National University Press, 1985). He has served as a consultant to several corporations, including Lucky-Goldstar, Daewoo, Samsung, Sunkyong, Hyundai, Kumho, and others, and has been a visiting professor at the Graduate School of Management at the University of California, Los Angeles.

Gerardo R. Ungson is associate professor of management in the Graduate School of Management at the University of Oregon. He received his Ph.D. from Pennsylvania State University and is the author of three books and a variety of articles focusing on decision-making, executive compensation, and international competition in the high-technology industry. His most recent book is *Competitive Strategies in High Technology: Meeting Institutional, Strategic, and Organizational Challenges* (Lexington, Mass.: D. C. Heath, 1990). Professor Ungson has served on the editorial boards of the *Academy of Management Review* and the *Journal of High Technology Management Research* and has been a consultant to several international high technology companies. He has served as visiting professor at the University of California, Berkeley; Dartmouth College, and Nijenrode, The Netherlands School of Business.